BOLD
moves

PIPPA HALLAS

CEO of Ella Baché

BOLD
moves

How to stand up,
step out and
make your next
bold move

WILEY

First published in 2019 by John Wiley & Sons Australia, Ltd
42 McDougall St, Milton Qld 4064

Office also in Melbourne

Typeset in 12.5/18pt Bembo Std

© John Wiley & Sons Australia, Ltd 2019

The moral rights of the author have been asserted

A catalogue record for this book is available from the National Library of Australia

Cover Design: Jennifer El-Chah, Loved.Locked.Loaded.

Printed in Singapore by C.O.S. Printers Pte Ltd

10 9 8 7 6 5 4 3 2 1

Disclaimer

The material in this publication is of the nature of general comment only, and does not represent professional advice. It is not intended to provide specific guidance for particular circumstances and it should not be relied on as the basis for any decision to take action or not take action on any matter which it covers. Readers should obtain professional advice where appropriate, before making any such decision. To the maximum extent permitted by law, the author and publisher disclaim all responsibility and liability to any person, arising directly or indirectly from any person taking or not taking action based on the information in this publication.

Dedicated to Ella Baché and Edith Hallas—two women who, with their individual approach, pioneering spirit and depth of understanding revolutionised the approach to skin. They taught us how to think, to care and above all to continue to learn.

CONTENTS

PREFACE

Ella's life was full with loving, eating and creating!
Edith Hallas

This is a book for you if, like me, you want to celebrate living a bold life filled with ordinary and extra-ordinary moments. It all starts with those first steps. Bold, for me, means a rich and abundant life, although not in a monetary sense. It means a life full of adventure, full of new experiences, and full of lots of life lessons and risk-taking. It means a life unique to me. Bold is when you feel the fear and don't always know how it's going to turn out. Living out of your comfort zone and doing it anyway. Seeing self-doubts as the norm and breaking through that voice in your head that tries to stop you.

As CEO of Ella Baché, and Ella's great-niece, plus a mum of two young boys, I'd like to help you discover how to own the skin you're in … how to own your story … and what it takes to show up again and again to fight for something you believe in. Our skin is so much more than how the world sees us: it's a reflection of our story. And it's my pleasure to tell the Ella Baché story—the person, the product and the brand—for the first time.

To uncover what it really takes to show up and own your story, to push through in moments of self-doubt and to live a life playing at the highest level, I interviewed some audacious Australian women: women who know that being bold takes passion, courage and focus and means pushing yourself outside your comfort zone, challenging the status quo and breaking down barriers and perceptions.

It doesn't mean you need to see yourself as a bold person, just an ordinary person who wants to follow their passion and make the most out of their life. You'll find these interviews between the chapters of this book, each one its own inspiring story of a bold woman.

I'm not bolder than anyone else. I have learned that making bold moves takes a lot of courage, a lot of focus and a lot of discipline. I don't see myself as a really disciplined person by any means. And I actually don't see myself as a bold person. I see myself as being like anyone else, but I'm also a person on a mission. I tend to be very stubborn and obsessive when I want to achieve something. In fact 'stubborn' is

Our skin is so much more than how the world sees us: it's a reflection of our story.

how my mum described me when I was growing up and I believe stubbornness has really helped me stick to the path that I'm on. The more often people have said 'no', the more motivated I've become. I'm passionate about what I do and have always been very single-minded about it.

Have I bitten off more than I can chew? That's a question that pops up in my mind every day, as I'm sure it does for anyone having to make daily bold decisions. But going for it anyway and backing yourself is where the magic happens. It's where the learnings occur, and sharing my doubts, mistakes and challenges with others has helped me along the way.

So this is not a book about how brave or bold I am—or how bold or brave anyone around me is for that matter. Rather, it's about what I've experienced on my journey in life so far and discovering what defined my great-aunt Ella and several equally bold Australian women. It's about what it takes to keep showing up when things gets tough. It's about the choices we have, how we make decisions based on those choices and the things we focus on. It's also about the people we choose to have in our lives; why the bold moves are frightening, scary and full of risk; and how they present us with such a fear of failing that it can lead to a shift in our mindset and goals.

You see, being paralysed by the fear of failure often prevents you from living your best life and, after all, we only get one crack at it. As women, we have a tendency to feel the need to wait for that perfect moment and to undo a lot of the deep-seated stereotypes we've carried with us from when we were young, such as 'being seen but not heard'. This is why I want to share the story of Ella Baché—what she has taught me and the lessons I learned by making bold decisions—in the hope that it will make it easier for others to do the same. Living a bold life means owning your actions—that's the good news. The bad news is that there's no silver bullet.

This is not a business book or even a leadership book; you can be an artist, a writer, an entrepreneur, a business leader, a teacher or a mum to benefit from reading it. Each chapter offers reflections and tips to inspire you to be bold in both your personal and professional life. Bold is a very personal thing: it means living outside your comfort zone, experiencing the lessons, the luck that comes from taking risks, the learnings and the growth. I've always tried to push myself out of my comfort zone and stretch myself

Living a bold life means owning your actions.

because I'm passionate about learning and curious about new things. I often question why I put this pressure on myself—why I don't just take the easy road and play it safe. The answer is 'Why not?' You only get one shot at it, so why not make it the best life you possibly can?

While we're still a long way off a world of gender equality, women have also come a long way and I believe it's our time to take the bull by the horns, get out there and make changes. Even if it means working twice as hard as men for the same reward or being the only female voice in the room, we are at a tipping point in many countries around the world. Only the other day I came across the term 'glass cliff'. It's an expression used to describe situations where women are given leadership positions that no man would take on because they are destined to fail. Yet there are so many amazing examples where women didn't fall off the cliff; they did the opposite and made it work. And they made it work because they worked harder, sacrificed more, had great networks around them that they had spent years building, and had a belief.

Our skin tells a story. From sun-kissed trips to the beach, to life-defining moments. The story of Ella Baché—a beautiful heritage brand, a product and a woman who recognised that each person's skin is individual—stretches back to 1936, across the oceans, to the streets of Paris, where Madame Baché had a revolutionary idea to appreciate every woman (and her skin) as an individual. Nearly 100 years later, with the same passion and desire for teaching women to learn to love the skin they're in that Ella Baché had all those years ago, I'll share with you on these pages Ella's story, my story and those of several remarkably bold Australian women.

Because in the end, it's about choice. Although we may not always control what happens in life — and yes, we all go through unexpected bad times and wonder how we'll ever make it through — we can control how we respond. What decisions are you making today? Are you making them boldly? How are you responding to situations?

We all have times in our lives where we need to make decisions: some simple, and some complex. To leave your country, to leave your relationship, to jump or not, to stay or go ... and to show up again and again.

When you've had a taste of the excitement, passion and confidence that can come from new experiences and learnings, you find there's only one option and that's the life you choose to lead when you get that fire in your belly. There is no other choice. Not making bold moves means we often play it safe and we miss out on opportunities that come from feeling uncomfortable. Yet it's these experiences that teach us the most — and that's where the magic happens!

I'm thrilled to be sharing with you my family's story and the Ella Baché story, as well as the journeys of other bold women, and the decisions they made along the way that became an integral part of their stories, to help you step out and live a bold life.

Pippa Hallas

INTRODUCING MADAME BACHÉ

We all have women who came before us. Those who we learned from, whose stories we listened to, and who shaped us in ways we never know. This is mine.

Ella Baché: a person, a product, a pioneer of the skincare industry and a household name synonymous with skincare results. Ella had a love for life as a pharmaceutical chemist and she had a great love for creating products. She was highly intelligent and no-nonsense. She grew up at a time when women were generally not educated and most did not work. Despite this, she obtained a university degree and had the foresight to leave Eastern Europe and travel to Paris in the 1920s, where she observed that French women were starting to take care of their skin. It was this observation that propelled her to create formulas that worked—rather than selling a 'miracle' product—building a reputation and a new life for herself.

The early years

Ella Baché Brummer, whose maiden name was Laszlo, was my great-aunt. She was born in Czechoslovakia in 1900 and enjoyed a happy childhood, but her life changed completely when she was in her twenties. After finishing school, she applied to study medicine, like her brother had, only to be denied a university place because she was a woman. Never one to be easily deterred, at the age of 26 Ella became the first woman to graduate as a pharmacist in Prague.

Ella was fortunate in that her family believed strongly in education, which gave her a broad perspective on life and world events. It was the 1920s, a time of uncertainty for Eastern Europe. World War I had ended, but there was tension in the air for many years—an uncertainty that was to culminate in World War II. Ella decided to leave her home country to seek a better life, and was never to return. She arrived in Paris with a degree in cosmetic chemistry only to realise it wasn't valid and she couldn't set up a business and work for herself as she had hoped. But that didn't stop Ella.

Not only did she leave her family behind when she moved to Paris, Ella also left behind a marriage. You see, Ella had entered into an arranged marriage with Mr Baché, a Viennese solicitor, whom she despised for his drinking and gambling.

On arriving in Paris with a bit of money she had been given as a wedding present, Ella started divorce proceedings immediately. I don't know anyone else who has used a wedding present to fund their divorce! (Then again, nor do I know anyone who has been trapped in an arranged marriage.)

Ella was determined to be in control of her own destiny and not be an employee, especially after her first marital experience—a bold move, I think, for a woman in the 1920s. So, there she was... in a new city...with no family and no networks...newly divorced...and with little money...during one of the most disruptive periods in history.

The hard work

Forging her own path as a cosmetic chemist in an era when women were competing with male domination, Ella had to rely on her own principles and tenacity. She was humble, proud and intellectual, and without an ego. She wasn't driven by money or fame but by her love of science. As there were no positions available for women in her field, she had to make her own.

This was a time when women were becoming increasingly aware of their skin. It was a time when many iconic pioneers of the industry were starting out in Paris. Realising there was an opportunity to develop her own scientific skincare products, Ella embarked on a career in pharmacy. She created her own skincare formulas from a tiny apartment in Rue de la Paix and then carried them, on foot, to local pharmacies.

It was also in the 1920s that Ella spent time with Edith, my grandmother, who was fondly known as 'Dixie'. The uneasy times had also led her to leave Eastern Europe. This move was to change the course of their lives forever on many levels.

So, Ella—the pharmacist—and Dixie—who was a beauty therapist—committed themselves to understanding all they could about our largest organ: the skin. They were both incredibly contemporary women. They were free spirits who developed an absolute respect for each other's knowledge and intellect and formed a very close relationship. The connection that these two women shared enabled them to reach a successful professional relationship very quickly. Dixie's passion and life obsession was nature, creation and the living cell. She would talk for hours about the skin's cells. Ella's approach was pharmaceutical, whereas Dixie's was all about the skin's needs. They had both always believed in making things happen, turning their goals into reality. Dixie often said, 'In the present, the future is not ours. And the moment the future becomes ours, it turns into the present'. They created a lifelong partnership and the rest, as they say, is history.

Their products would revitalise skin cells, improve elasticity and provide antibacterial protection. Ella endeavoured to personalise products—it wasn't about one size fits all, it was about tailoring products and treatments for individual skins.

In 1936 Ella opening her own store. Today, this store, located under her apartment, still stands. Ella was outgoing, generous and warm-hearted, but she was also tough when it came to running her business. If she hadn't been, it would never have survived. Her employees respected her and she didn't tolerate fools.

From Paris to New York

Ella's story was destined to change again when, in 1940, the Nazis invaded France, forcing her to leave everything she had worked for. She fled to Portugal and from there journeyed by ship to New York City, where her brother and his wife lived, handing over her company in Paris to Lucy Anndero, one of her staff members.

On Ella's first night in New York she was invited to a dinner where she was introduced to a well-known art collector, Ernest Brummer, who would become her second husband. At the beginning of their relationship they lived together unmarried, later moving to Madison Avenue, where they lived on one floor while Ernest occupied the second floor with his gallery. Ella focused on her work and set up a laboratory on 55th Street, which she walked to each day.

Ella and Ernest always held separate bank accounts. This is just one bold move that shows how Ella—as a female businesswoman in New York—used her tenacity and stubbornness to shift people's perception of women in business. As always, her great focus and intellect put her in good stead to run a business.

Opening a laboratory in New York enabled Ella to continue with her research and product development while formulating new products and sending them back to Paris for manufacturing. Ella's Parisian laboratory, 'Suzy', was in Rue Godot de Mauroy. She never disclosed why she named the laboratory 'Suzy', but it still remains as the trademark today. Ella maintained the highest standards—she could tell through touch alone how effective a product was.

The legacy

After the war, Ella would travel back and forth between New York and her apartment in Paris. She spent many evenings with her best friend, Yvonne, who was one of the first female lawyers in France. Yvonne worked to defend female rights and focused her career on human rights, women's rights and justice—a topic that is still as relevant today as it was in the 1960s.

In a world where women were not allowed in boardrooms, Ella spoke French, German, Czech and Hungarian and would often be heard debating and discussing world issues and the rights of women to the people around her.

When Ella Laszlo Baché Brummer died in 1999, *The New York Times* did not print an obituary. Women and people of colour were systematically denied such rights. This was despite the fact that Ella had founded a company with stores in 22 countries, and invented countless breakthroughs in the skincare/beauty business.

In 2018, *The New York Times* recognised that obituaries were predominantly dominated by white men, and the paper has now decided to include women of Ella's era. It's just the beginning of what I remain hopeful is a movement recognising the power of women!

Ella's legacy was her deep understanding of our skin and the treatments needed to overcome skin problems. However, what many people don't know is that after her husband, Ernest Brummer, died Ella gave five years of her life to documenting and bequesting Ernest's world-famous and very valuable art collection. Much of it is now found at the 'Met' museum of art in New York, where as recently as 2017 there was an exhibition of Ernest's work that Ella had previously put together.

Ella was simple, uncomplicated, no-nonsense and decisive. People expect a family of high fashion and makeup. My memories of Ella were of her long, straight, dark-brown hair pulled back in a bun or plaits. There was no time for makeup or hours of grooming; life was there to be lived.

Ella lived an extraordinary life defined by world events out of her control. She responded with bold moves, allowing her to determine her own destiny and not allowing anyone else to write her story. She had to be bold and if she could be bold despite all the obstacles that stood in her way, then we can too.

Ella certainly didn't build her success on fads or trends, vanity or makeup, or her Instagram life. She was comfortable with who she was—in her own skin and in control of her destiny—and with her uncomplicated, decisive, no-nonsense manner she mastered the needs of the skin in a loving, passionate and unforgiving way.

Ella had to be bold and if she could be bold despite all the obstacles that stood in her way, then we can too.

Today, Ella Baché is a global skincare brand and if Madame Baché were still alive, she would be extremely humbled by it and not at all interested in any fanfare.

Chapter 1
OWN YOUR STORY

Because no two skins are alike
Madame Baché

What does it take to show up and decide to own your story?

My story has been passed down from generation to generation. All of ours have. But this is my unique story and one that has become synonymous with skin—healthy individual skin is at the heart of it—and for the first time I want to share this message of ownership and acceptance with a new generation of women.

Backing your intuition

Across the oceans, in Paris, is where my story began when I found myself, on a sunny spring morning in May 1999, sitting by the Opéra National de Paris. I had been in Paris nearly a year and felt it was time to decide what was next. Where should I go? Should I go alone? What was the next step in my career? I was craving

1

clarity. I'd been given the opportunity to spend a year in Paris in my great-aunt Ella Baché's apartment, where she had lived, when she wasn't in New York, from the 1920s to 1990s.

I thought a lot about the crossroads she faced in her life and the crossroads I was now facing in mine. I was born in Sydney, Australia, and was blessed with a free-range childhood, which I changed for adventure and out of choice. As you would have read in the introduction to this book, Ella also enjoyed a happy childhood but the change in her life story was quite different from mine.

Ella's life change was about making choices for survival, whereas mine was about making choices for myself. Ella would never return home. I could go home to Australia any time I wanted. A place I loved: a place where I had strong networks, friends and family. And the world wasn't facing the biggest disruption of all time. I just needed to be bold, decide what my next move was going to be and follow my heart regardless of what other people thought. I'd figured out that sometimes this meant letting go, even if it involved leaving a comfortable situation for the unknown.

Before arriving in Paris I had spent a few years working in advertising in London after finishing my degree in business marketing back in Sydney. I loved marketing and communications. I loved understanding what makes people tick—how to initiate communication to engage a positive response. I loved taking in as much information as possible, making the complex simple and using it to understand and change behaviours in a positive way. I had never understood why people make things more complex than they need to be, even in the most complex of situations. I loved people and understanding what they are made of. So travelling, meeting new people and being exposed to new cultures was perfect for me. I had a wonderful Australian boyfriend, with whom I had travelled, but he was in Edinburgh, working.

So I had come to Paris on my own—barely speaking a word of French—and gone to work in Ella's factory, which was still in the suburbs of Paris at that time, while living in her apartment at No. 8 Rue de la Paix. Although my situation was very different from Ella's, we both lived in this little apartment in Paris at completely different times.

I had decisions to make. Should I return to Sydney to work in my family's business, Ella Baché, which had become one of Australia's most loved and known skincare brands, or should I continue my career in advertising? Should I continue my relationship with my boyfriend and settle down, or did I need to be single and free: to find out more about myself and what I was supposed to be doing?

After a few years of living overseas, I decided it was time to make my way back home to Sydney to see my family. As soon as I arrived I knew it was time to start afresh. My boyfriend and I would go our separate ways. I would take the leap into the Hallas family business: Ella Baché.

I have always had a philosophy and attitude that if something doesn't excite me and doesn't make a difference in my life—a new, fun experience, where I can give it my best shot and that I can put my all into—I would move on to the next thing. I say 'yes' more often than 'no', even when I don't exactly know how I'm going to do something, and at times I have certainly landed on my face. Some people think it's been easy for me because I have the backing of my family and my family's business, and my response is yes, that's true—to a degree. I have had wonderful opportunities and role models, but they certainly wouldn't have been there if I hadn't made certain decisions, put everything on the line and made scarifies along the way. Hard work, persistence, determination, 'jumping' and saying *yes!* (I don't take 'no' from anyone easily) is definitely in my DNA. When it gets overwhelming and I think maybe I've bitten off more than I can chew I always remind myself to 'come back to the moment'. Break it down and compartmentalise my thoughts, follow my intuition—it's always right. As Brené Brown once said, 'You either walk inside your story and own it or you stand outside your story and hustle for your worthiness'.

Owning your decisions

I was born two months prematurely and the doctor told my parents that I would be extremely determined because only the determined survive such an early birth (especially all those decades ago). I obviously can't remember what it was like for those first few months, but I know it was tough for my mum, especially as a first-time parent. Nature or nurture is often discussed, and while I think both define you as a person, your work ethic definitely comes from your parents. They were your first role models. So, fighting for my life from the beginning and having strong, hardworking role models, I was destined to work hard and make work an important part of my life.

I've had so many moments where my head and heart have certainly not matched what I've shown to the world, and sometimes they still don't. There's a moment like that, probably every day of my life. On the outside I can come across very much in control and poised, but on the inside I'm questioning myself the whole time.

But, it's through experience that you get a bit bolder every time you do something. I think the more you do it, the easier it does get as you push yourself to exceed the next challenge. I own the decisions I've made and they have been influenced by the strong women in my family.

I have often thought over the years, why I chose to live this story. What is my purpose? Why do I work so hard at what I do? What am I supposed to give others? It's the fire in my belly that drives me to keep striving to do things better, to create and build, to fix and solve problems. I have always been a fixer: if something needs fixing, I will be there. It's not always the right thing to be. I have learned I can't fix everything. That's a hard lesson. But I will keep pushing hard for what needs to be done, if it's

It's through experience that you get a bit bolder every time you do something.

the right thing to do. Once you own your story, no-one else will—not your parents, your kids, your colleagues—only you. So live the experiences, own your decisions and remain realistic about the life you have chosen to lead. Taking ownership of your decisions, your story or whatever it may be in your life means you are taking the responsibility and turning it into a journey.

It's how we respond to these experiences that shapes our story. I wanted to share my story so others open up and share theirs. And by sharing my story, I hope others will share theirs and believe anything is possible.

Discovering my ancestry in Paris

Spending time in Paris was my opportunity to experience a new culture: to be inspired by art, people and a different way of doing things. To enjoy the finer aspects of Parisian life. Travel always reinvigorates my soul; it broadens my mind and gives me new inspiration and ideas. I was living in Ella's apartment in one of the most magical streets of Paris where Ella had lived above her original salon, which still exists today. I felt blessed to have this opportunity: to not only experience Paris but also be given the chance to revisit my family's heritage. Paris is a romantic city. A city so easy to fall in love with for its history, charm, style, food and way of life. I had loved living in London too, for different reasons. But when I arrived in Paris I instantly felt the change of pace: it didn't have the hustle and bustle of London.

Travel always reinvigorates my soul; it broadens my mind and gives me new inspiration and ideas.

I arrived on the Eurostar with my backpack and headed to the Ella Baché salon to pick up the key to the apartment that I would call home for the next year. The skin therapists working in the salon didn't know who I was, or why I was there, but they were lovely and helped me into my new home. They were used to Australians coming to visit as the brand is so well known. (They would later ask me, why do so many Australians visit us and why do they know so much about their skin and the products?) My French was terrible, and being there alone was a little overwhelming, but it didn't seem to matter. People had time, they made the effort if you did and I easily adapted to life alone and created a daily routine for myself.

Ella's apartment was in the heart of the city on the right bank, just up the street from the famous Ritz Hotel. It is a wide street flanked by old-style apartments with Juliette balconies, high ceilings, tiny kitchenettes, old metal lifts and enormous charm. It was amazing to sleep in Ella's bed, stand on the Juliette balcony and watch the world pass by. The only thing left in Ella's apartment (she lived in the US for the last 10 years of her life) was a big, old-worldly cupboard in the lounge room. It had two large drawers at the bottom and I opened one of them to find a pile of black-and-white photos—nothing else. It turned out these photos had been taken by my dad in the 1960s during a student uprising in Paris. Again, history continues through the generations.

I established my routine in Paris. I tried to start my day with some exercise, which I quickly realised is not the Parisian way. I would walk and jog the streets of Paris early in the morning trying hard not to get lost while searching for a yoga class, gym or swimming pool. They just didn't exist! I even went as far as asking if I could use the pool at the Ritz to do early morning laps. It was a no-go.

The French don't love exercise like the Aussies do. So walking turned out to be the best form of movement. I quickly learned how much of the beautiful city you could see on foot. After my morning walk I would go to a little café downstairs from the apartment and stand at the bar for my morning espresso, trying my best to talk French to the barista. Next I'd jump on a train for Monterey, in the suburbs of Paris, where the Ella Baché head office and factory were. I would spend my day there adding as much value as I could to the team, with the little French I had. We would go out to lunch at a local restaurant every day and I soon learned that not eating meat was also very un-French!

Despite my communication difficulties and not loving heavy, meaty meals, I did my best not to be an Aussie outsider. After work I would often meet up with my new French artist friends, who a friend in London had introduced me to. They became my tribe and family while I was in France. We would go to art galleries, exhibitions and dinners and we had an amazing time exploring Paris. I am fortunate that I have always found it easy to meet people and create relationships. So even when I travelled and lived in new places on my own, I never found myself alone for long. My time in Paris gave me a deeper understanding of the French way of life and why it was the birthplace of so many luxury things. They know how to value the good things in life. I loved my year in Paris and I was sure I would go back and live there again one day.

Following your path

I always knew I wasn't going to be a scientist like Ella and her cousin — my grandmother — Edith (Dixie) Hallas. In fact, I didn't even study science at school. I wasn't into it at all. I was more of an extrovert. I loved people. I loved understanding what makes people tick, how to influence people through communication and change behaviour for the good. I loved the creative process and I also loved economics (I think that was because I had a great teacher). I didn't follow Ella's path into the field of science, but would later follow her path into the family business.

When I look back and reflect on my story, or even Ella's for that matter, I can't help but notice the major life-changing milestones that shaped both of our stories: some by design, some responding to the events out of our control. Even at times when I don't know where I'm going, or how I'm going to get there, I just choose to say 'yes' instead of 'no'. My decisions aren't always the right ones—both personally and professionally—but I make them, so I need to own them.

My Ella Baché story is part of my life journey, and I feel very fortunate and grateful to be leading a business and a brand that is part of my family's heritage. I'm not a CEO in a top-100 company who's telling someone else's story—or a made-up story—to give the company warmth. This is a *real* story, and it's about *real* people, and I'm very proud of having had Ella and Dixie—strong, innovative, pioneering women—as role models in my own family, but also in the business. Ella's and Dixie's story is detailed in the introduction to this book, if you haven't already read it!

So I wanted to share their story—their beliefs and their philosophies—with you. They weren't businesspeople. They weren't marketers. They were creators and innovators. They were scientists, at the end of the day. So, I've unpacked and worked to understand a lot of that science, putting a relevant spin on it so we can protect the magic and heritage of Ella Baché and take it into the future.

Determining your focus

Ella didn't have any children. I'm not sure why, because she loved my brother and me, my dad (her nephew) and her other great-nieces and -nephews. I always knew I wanted to have children, but I also knew I wanted to work as well. I was lucky to find role models in Ella and Dixie, who could teach me how to do both.

One of the things that stops people I meet from living a bold life and really owning their story—and I know this was true for my own mum, and for a lot of women I know—is the fear that if they start to step out there and step into this 'big thing', it will take away from their time with people who matter to them.

That it would take away from their children…their partners…everyone in their world. I don't believe that. I believe everyone has a big capacity and a lot to give and there is enough to go around.

I believe everyone has a big capacity and a lot to give and there is enough to go around.

When I had my second child, I was worried it would take away from my first child. My mum said to me, 'It doesn't work like that. You just multiply the love that you have to give and you have enough for everyone'.

Everyone's definition of living a bold life and everyone's story is different. So, this is my own personal view on it. I know I'm a better person, and a better mum, and a better wife, and a better friend if I'm doing what I do and what I love. I don't see any costs associated with it. Yes, of course there are sacrifices, but I don't see them as costs. If my kids need me I'm there. I would never sacrifice their needs.

Today, I have two boys aged six and three. I am the CEO of Ella Baché and every day I just try and do my best. The days are ridiculously full and I constantly have to check myself, as living every day at full capacity can be far from ideal.

I'm domestically hopeless, but then again that's not where I put my energy. The dishwasher gets stacked like it's origami; I lose my keys; leave the doors of the house open and I'm always looking for that missing library book! Thankfully, my family looks after me on that front. But I do get quite obsessive about my kids' homework and projects—just as I do with my work. Lachie, my older son, has a 'News' session every week at school. It's a news presentation and update. I have to pull myself back with it because I get just as single-minded with his homework as I do with my work. It's my personality. My husband says to me, 'Can we stop working on Peter Rabbit?' (or whatever the news topic is for that week).

But my story is that I co-parent with my husband so our kids don't miss out and we both don't miss out. I don't believe men want to be chained to their desk all day and never see their kids either (like they did in the 1970s and 1980s). I feel like they have an equally loving relationship with their dad, and that's really important to us. And they also have equally loving relationships with many people in their lives. After all, it takes a village, right? This is only the first generation of co-parenting, so only time will tell how it impacts our kids, but for now it works for us.

You always bring your own experience to situations. So I bring my experience in my own life from both of my parents to my own parenting. I grew up in an open-door household. We always had lots of people around us, and I had a few amazing people, who weren't my mum and dad, in my childhood who taught me a lot. So, for me it's about setting my life and my kids' lives up by ensuring time with friends, and other quality relationships, the best way I can. The definition of family is so much broader than just your dad and mum.

Owning your story and making bold decisions is always going to include a massive gap between coming up with a vision of something (an exercise plan, a business—whatever it is that you're looking to create), getting it clear in your head, and saying it out loud for the first time, and actually making the vision a reality.

If you follow your heart and your passion, your energy will bring people along with you. Ensuring you stay focused, and determining what your passion and focus is versus the noise is what's important. Quite often the noise will be people projecting their own fears onto you, so it's not about you at all but rather it's about them. I saw an awesome quote by Elon Musk that read, 'Pay attention to the signal and not the noise'. Tune into the signal—what's true for you, your instincts, ideas—and cut out the noise.

Tune into the signal — what's true for you, your instincts, ideas — and cut out the noise. I'm lucky in that I'm able to focus and cut out the noise, no matter what I'm doing. Even at university, I could sit in a corner of the room with a party going on, and finish my homework. If I didn't want to miss out on what was going on, I would try and do both together.

I have always been very single-minded about chasing what I want and living my story. I don't do things by halves. I try to believe in myself and listen to myself. But when it comes to being heard by others, it's a different story! And that's the topic of the next chapter.

BE BOLD
AND OWN YOUR STORY

If you are fortunate enough to find your role model and your passion, dig deep: be bold and find what it takes to show up and really own your story. Here's a list to reflect on.

* Find an amazing role model.

* Back yourself and your intuition.

* Find and follow your passion.

* Follow your heart.

* Stand in the personal highs and lows, and choose how you respond to the tough times so you can get yourself off the floor.

* Own your decisions and have the courage to follow your own path. Sometimes this involves sacrifices and trade-offs.

* Live *your* life—sometimes that means letting go of things.

* Own your story by standing in your own space and not someone else's.

* Look out for opportunities and moments of luck. They exist, so grab them with both hands!

TALKING BOLD AND OWNING YOUR STORY
WITH LORNA JANE CLARKSON

Alongside both mine and Ella's story, I wanted to discover what drives some of Australia's most audacious women to live a bold life: what makes them tick and what drives them to do what they do every day.

We all know the term 'active wear'. It describes the global phenomenon of fashionable workout wear that transcends the gym and yoga studios into everyday life—but did you know that an Aussie invented it?

Frustrated by the dull, ill-fitting and uninspiring range of gym wear available for women, Lorna Jane Clarkson took matters into her own hands. She started sewing outfits while working as a gym instructor in 1989 with the desire of celebrating women's bodies and encouraging active living as a positive lifestyle choice, rather than being focussed on weight loss. Her designs quickly gained a following. Today, the Lorna Jane brand stands for so much more than active wear and Lorna now shares her personal practice of 'Move. Nourish. Believe.' This is what she had to say about her journey.

★ ★ ★

It took 25 years for me to convince women to start wearing Activewear in their everyday lives—and I really believe that it's my passion to inspire women, focus and bold moves that made it happen.

To me, living a bold life is the only way to live and happens when you decide to take control of your life and you live it on your own terms guided by your own set of principles and beliefs. I think it's harder to do today than ever before as we are all so influenced by social media and have become preoccupied with what other people are doing. It worries me that we're becoming too busy watching other people's lives to find the time and energy to work on our own!

Being bold is essential if you want to create a life that you love and it takes a whole lot of determination, courage, focus and an unwavering belief in yourself.

My boldest move (and I think one of my first) would have to be the day I quit the security of my full-time job to start making Activewear, a category that didn't even exist at the time. People thought I was crazy and they weren't afraid to tell me. But you know what, maybe a little bit of crazy is exactly what you need to go against popular opinion and find the courage to make your bold move!

I think what stops people boldly going after their dreams is mostly their fear of failure. Living a bold life is about accepting the fact that failure is part of the process and it WILL happen. We need to become comfortable with making mistakes and looking a little foolish along the way, because when you set out to try something new it's the mistakes that teach us the lessons that ultimately get us to where we want to be!

As a business owner and entrepreneur, it's my job to make sure my brand doesn't stand still, which requires me to make bold moves time and time again. I've learned to enjoy the energy rush that comes with trying new things because it means that I'm moving my business forward. I think you need to get comfortable with a higher level of intensity in everything that you do if you want to live a bold life and be successful. But it's comforting to know that as time goes by it doesn't feel so intense because you somehow become used to it and what used to be 'intense' becomes your new normal.

Over the years I've learned that when it comes to making decisions about my life and my business the best person to make them is ME! I've become more confident being myself because I realise that there are people who will love me and my brand and then there are others who won't — and I'm okay with that. I also understand that this confidence in myself has come through experience and seeing the difference it makes to me and my business when I back myself. Sometimes my decisions work out perfectly and sometimes they don't — but for every misstep there's a lesson to be learnt that makes me better than I was before. Being true to myself and my vision for Lorna Jane is important to me because when you spend too much time listening to and comparing yourself to other people, you ultimately dilute your message and what you and your brand stand for.

When I started Lorna Jane and invented the Activewear category as we know it today, I had a goal and that was to inspire women to be active in pieces they could wear in their everyday life. It was a bold idea — something that took me over 25 years to achieve and something I am extremely proud of.

Active wear is a huge industry now, larger than so many imagined it could be. But I believe that it's only just the beginning and my journey is far from over. I have no doubt that there will be a lot more decisions that require me to be bold and back myself. Because I know without a doubt that it's not just one, but a series of bold moves that makes our lives the exciting and rewarding adventure it should be!

Chapter 2
OWN YOUR VOICE

The trouble is, you think you have more time.
Buddha

D
o you own your voice?

If you had 20 seconds of 'insane courage'—a term coined by Benjamin Mee of *We Bought a Zoo* renown—what would you do?

What would you say? What's holding you back?

If you want to be bold, you need to find your voice and figure out where you need to be heard so you can really make an impact and a difference.

When I first started working at Ella Baché there were so many moments where I didn't feel I was being heard. I was misunderstood and I certainly didn't get the traction I had expected (and had received in the past). In fact, I had no voice, I had no credibility and in those early years I faced countless barriers that prevented me from owning my voice and being heard. I had to stand up, pick my battles, play the long game and show up time and time again. It took insane courage.

Being unique

The most common question I get asked is 'Did you always plan to work for Ella Baché?' The answer is *no!*

Back in the 1990s my brother and I would spend days and weeks of our school holidays in the Ella Baché factory or manufacturing plant in Sydney. The wonderful part of this is that some of the people we used to work with back then are still there today. On a Monday morning we would turn up at around 8.30 am and most people had already been there for hours. I would sit on a stool in front of a big, long white bench and be tasked with folding cartons and putting jars into the cartons, which I then placed into boxes. I always worked at the fastest possible pace so I could get out of there earlier than I was meant to. I had one eye on a magazine, reading about the latest in fashion and beauty, and the other on one of our dogs sitting beside me (of course that wouldn't happen today with all the regulations). I like to remind my dad that he still owes me for those hours and hours of working in the warehouse, but I never complained, especially after seeing my grandma and grandpa work tirelessly on the brand. My grandpa (who was Ella's cousin) was a lawyer and an accountant. He was a lovely, warm man, but he was tough on us. He was highly educated, spoke seven languages and was a refugee from Czechoslovakia. He never spent a cent on himself as he had lived through the Great Depression. At the end of my working day at the warehouse I would often walk into his office to see him sitting at his large, wooden desk and report back on what I had done that day and how I was going at school.

The day I turned 16 I started driving, and a year later, on my seventeenth birthday, I earned the freedom to drive on my own. Being a poor student, I never had enough money to fill the car up with petrol, so I took advantage of the family's account at the local petrol station down the road from the office (the accounts consisted of handwritten file cards in a box on the counter!). For months I thought I'd been able to get away with it. But then one day I walked into my grandpa's office and he confronted me with the monies I owed the company for the petrol I had used. I never did that again!

Fast-forward to 2005: I had taken the leap into the world of advertising. I had an amazing time, working hard and playing hard in advertising in both Sydney and London. I loved every minute of it and met some incredible people along the way. Working with such inspiring people, I built a strong comradeship with them; it was as though we had grown up together. We were fortunate enough to create some amazing experiences and breakthrough ideas together; before the business world began using buzz words such as 'differentiation' and 'breakthrough thinking and ideas' this was our ethos. Along the way, we had some really difficult clients and some really kind ones, but it taught us to deal with different people: to negotiate, influence, persuade, collaborate and solve problems. I managed a variety of accounts, both for-profit and not-for-profit, working on pitches until all hours of the morning and achieving some great wins and also some hard losses. It was all part of the game and something that provided me with much growth.

My career so far, I acknowledged, was abundant—but the advertising world was a young person's game, especially for females. I had two female bosses in the Sydney agencies I worked for. They worked hard and were often in the office until after

9 pm, fighting for a seat at the table because, as women, they were the minority and that was a tough place to be. I knew it wasn't an industry for women over 35 who wanted to have a family but also had ambitions to continue to build a great career in something they truly loved.

Philosophically, if you're unique no-one can compete. Building a brand and standing out where competitors were large multinationals, you had to be different. The Ella Baché uniqueness came from Ella's approach towards treating the skin and the products, but also in the way the brand was taken to market with PR, advertising and events all used to differentiate and stand for something in a competitive marketplace. We had to create our own voice that no-one else could own. The personality of the brand has always been cheeky, quirky, polished, sophisticated, Australian, and of course, French. We have never told the family story as part of the brand story or put the family front and centre in the brand's story. But I've never had people say Ella *who?* Everyone knows Ella Baché: the brand, the company. But they don't know the person, the family or the human story—probably because fame and spotlight have always been the furthest thing from what my family values.

Believing in yourself

In my early thirties I had a conversation with my dad John, who was not only my father but also the owner and chairman of Ella Baché. I said to him that maybe it was time I thought about joining the family business because I was seriously considering jumping in and giving it a go. I was fortunate that we had always spoken about what was happening at Ella Baché and with the brand, so I knew it from afar and through his eyes. But, boy, I could never have imagined how challenging it was going to be. I was completely and utterly naive!

My dad lived on the north coast of New South Wales and although he owned the company, he hadn't been involved in the business day-to-day for over 20 years. So after 20 years of having no family members in the business, walking in with my surname freaked everyone out in more ways than I can even to this day comprehend—I felt as though I was a spy.

So, after years of building my credibility and career in advertising, I had to prove myself all over again. After years of owning my voice in the world of advertising, I had to reinvent myself. I think the toughest part of it was the alienation. Being a social person, I had always had lots of friends at work. So this was really tough. I was alienated by many of the managers at the time, and my peers were frightened that if they were perceived as being 'on my side' it wouldn't work out favourably for them.

I persevered because I strongly believed it was my right to be there and no-one was going to take that away from me. Even if I couldn't win the battle, I would win the war—this was a long-term game for me.

I spent three years heading up marketing at Ella Baché and I was very fortunate in that I had some great mentors outside of the business with whom I spent confidential and valuable time. If I was going to run the business one day—which by then I knew I wanted to do—I had to fill myself with ambition and like-minded people. I love the saying 'don't poke the bear': I knew that I would eventually get there through hard work, resilience, persistence and determination after having been the 'bear' who was poked so many times over for being part of the family. With people around me doubting me and my association with the brand making me even more determined, I just needed to use the time to learn more about the financial and manufacturing side of the business. With the support of my mentors, who I'm still very close with today, I set out to do just that behind the scenes.

Holding on to your values

In 2009, just as the GFC hit, I got my chance to take on the role of CEO of Ella Baché. The media headlines were all doom and gloom, the banks had collapsed overseas, people were losing their homes and everyone was fearful that we would head into a recession. Running a retail business, you rely a lot on consumer confidence and how people feel so it was a time of uncertainty, but I knew we had a great brand and if we held onto our principles and smarts we could ride this wave.

Nevertheless, it took me a while to comprehend the fact that the buck stopped with me. I'm not into titles, so that wasn't an issue, but I had to get my head around being the leader and not an imposter. Yet I suddenly found myself with imposter syndrome and there was no vitamin I could take to cure it—it was something I had to solve on my own. It's a strange feeling when you've had a job description—a road map—all your working life and all of a sudden you have none of that.

I was a 33-year-old female CEO, sitting in my office thinking, 'Okay, what do I do now?' I remember asking my dad, 'So what are your expectations?' Dad's reply was, 'Just do what you're doing, but more of it'—always supportive, but not one for the finer details!

First, there were changes to be made within the business. I believe life is too short to work with rattlesnakes so the first thing I needed to do was get my team together and build trust, honesty and commitment. Get the right people on the bus and the wrong people off. After that, I had to work out where it was we needed to go! If you have a passionate, hardworking team around you—one that you can trust, where everyone has each other's back—anything is possible.

The culture had to revert to embracing our family values. I knew exactly what they were, and how to get there. The company had been corporatised and was full of rules and policy. We had to go back to being free to innovate and collaborate—and not sweat the small things, like where you parked your car! I realised we had an identity crisis. Companies, like people, need to know who they are, what they stand for, what their strengths are and what their personality is. We quickly re-defined all of that. The values that Ella had brought to the business were innovation, bravery, pushing boundaries, working hard, creating good relationships and making people feel like family. All of these still applied and remain at the core of the brand. It was only natural to want to voice these values and embed them across the organisation. Fortunately, my first year as CEO was a great year. It was before I had kids so I worked seven days a week and extremely long hours. I was conscious that I had to make the role my own, and that meant doing things differently from how my dad, Ella or the leaders before me had done them.

Standing out from the rest

The impact of technology and the growth in digital were prevalent. We had to take what was good about the past and protect it while also making changes where necessary for the future and this meant leveraging the opportunities that the growth of the digital world presented—and it meant moving quickly. To this day I am conscious of the balancing act between the human touch and technology.

I often find myself faced with decisions and in those moments I draw on my knowledge of the principles and values that made the company great. I always reflect on Ella's philosophies and beliefs. I'm here for a moment in time to lead the company; I have always seen my role in the company as one of protecting what makes it great—its philosophies, values and heritage. It's about taking that heritage and building on the future.

Ella's pursuit was always to formulate quality and result-driven products using the best raw materials and to understand the properties of these natural materials, which were sourced from all over the world.

The formulas were crude—she pushed back on over-refined ingredients. To her it was like cooking with only the best ingredients. There's nothing new about this today—in fact, it's now normal for products to be formulated with vitamins, herbs, marine extracts, essential oils, proteins, biological extracts and tissue molecules. If the ingredients worked, Ella used them, with each ingredient serving its purpose. In a world of mass production and uniformity there was a need for an individual approach, which is what she delivered.

This went against the trends of producing light, water-based products. Instead, she used products with higher efficacy that *actually worked* to improve the skin, just as prescription formulas would. It was a bold move. It would have been easier to create products like other cosmetic companies did, but Ella didn't believe they had the same potential for results on the skin.

The prime example was her commitment to lanolin, which was a controversial ingredient. Lanolin can hold three times its own weight in water, making it a most effective moisturiser. Ella was committed to research on herbal-based products and would research native plants such as allantoin, which is used in indigenous environments, and comfrey, used by Indigenous American Indians. These ingredients, combined with scientific advances, were a true testament to Ella's uniqueness and individuality.

She invented these products after much research, documentation and observation of different cultures as well as exploration of the medicinal properties of the skin. With her knowledge she used the active principles to create a line of skincare rich in vitamins A, C and E that promised to provide antioxidant protection and essential nourishment, later combining jojoba, grapeseed and rosemary.

Ella always said 'no two skins are alike', and that's still our mantra today. Back in the 1920s she also pulled on many levers that as a CEO I need to pull on today. We are fortunate that advancements in technology have enabled us to go beyond the skin and products to take the idea of personalisation into how we communicate and service our clients. Ella had to build networks back in the 1920s; she created a reputation through different networks for her products and formulas. She did this by way of one-on-one relationships and was very strict about who she associated with. It was only people she respected. She was very principled.

Today, the Ella Baché network is much larger. We're fortunate that we have so many different platforms that we can use to build our network with: social media has revolutionised the way we do this. Like Ella, we knew we had to own our voice and stand out to get attention. While the competition was not nearly as great in the 1930s and the industry was at its infancy stage, Ella still had to gain attention and stand out among the rest. She achieved this by building a reputation for her products. She showed that they worked—that you could trust them and her genius formulations. Today, standing out and owning your voice is no different: only the way we go about it and the platforms we use are.

Being passionate

In the early days as CEO, I had a great opportunity to go on a show called *Undercover Boss*. I jumped at the chance because it not only profiled the company on national television, it also profiled some of the incredible people within our organisation. It heroed their stories and granted some of them an opportunity to follow their dreams, whether it was to travel to see their mum in another country or to write a book. I was able to go into the organisation as a trainee therapist and gain insights into what was going on, an opportunity I wouldn't have as CEO. I literally went undercover for a few weeks and travelled around to a dozen Ella Baché stores, where I worked 'undercover' in disguise. I got to see the wonderful things people were doing in all areas of the business. I also experienced an enormous amount of passion, ownership and love for the brand. As a CEO you often visit stores and people, but you experience it through a very different lens. The show gave me the opportunity to see the business from the inside out and to work alongside people I would never get the chance to as CEO.

The most challenging part of the show was when they asked me to go to our factory. Having worked there since I was a young kid I knew the staff like my own family. I knew they would recognise me—even wearing a disguise. So, despite the risk of my cover being blown, the TV crew took the chance and sent me there. Within five minutes of walking in, one of the ladies screamed 'Pippa what have you done to your hair?' My cover was blown and the segment never made it to air! Being part of *Undercover Boss* made me realise how many amazing women, some with hard-luck stories, are part of the Ella Baché family. It shows

'**Business is about people and the relationships you create around them.**'

how special and unique the passion, commitment and love for the brand is and is a reminder of how each of us has their own story.

We have an annual awards night where we award people within our network for their great achievements over the past year. The night is one of my favourite events as hundreds of people gather at a venue in Sydney to celebrate each other's achievements. You can't create this magic on a spreadsheet: it's built over many, many years of experience, hard work and relationships. As my dad would always say, 'business is about people and the relationships you create around them'.

Making a difference

As a brand, Ella Baché has always supported women and the belief that they deserve an equal go. It's part of the human spirit, but also the Aussie spirit of 'Have a go!' We're proud of our heritage and have fought for females to be given an equal start.

The 1990s was a time when 'ironmen'—who were celebrated for their speed and endurance—were our Aussie heroes and a big part of the Australian beach culture. Ella Baché worked with the Surf Life Saving Association in a bid to introduce an Australian ironwoman competition alongside the men's. At that time women didn't have a place in Australian sport and they certainly didn't have a place in the surf life-saving culture. The ironman event has been around since the 1960s, but it took three years, and hundreds of meetings with both state and federal bodies, to convince the Surf Life Saving Association in Australia to trial the first ironwoman event. It was a success! Today it's on a par with the men's event. The ironwoman event provided a platform for many talented female competitors to build a profile and go on to be serious sportspeople in their own rights.

One of the sponsorship events that put the Ella Baché brand in the hearts and minds of many Australians, especially men, was our involvement with the 18-foot Skiffs. At the time (the early 1990s) these were the fastest sailing boats on the water and the events were televised nationally during lunch break for the cricket. Ella Baché agreed to sponsor the boats on the proviso that we had a female skipper. This was a first for Australian Skiff racing. Adrienne Cahalan became the skipper for the Ella Baché 18-foot Skiff for the next seven years and went on to win many series. Adrienne, despite her petite, 47-kilogram frame, was the most mentally tough and strongest on the water. Adrienne is a champion cross-country skier, a musician and a maritime lawyer—a high achiever in everything she does. Like Adrienne, women who compete at the highest levels in a male-dominated environment need to be mentally strong, bold, focused and ambitious.

Our involvement with female skippers and sailing continued when, in 2011, we sponsored Jessica Watson. Jess assembled and skippered the youngest crew ever to race in the iconic Sydney to Hobart race, with sailors ranging in age from 17 to 21. Jess had just been named Young Australian of the Year after sailing solo around the world. (You'll find more on Jess's amazing achievements in the Talking Bold interview at the end of chapter 4.) But leading a team was a different experience. The crew trained hard for three months and lived together in a house on the northern beaches of New South Wales. It was like *Big Brother*, but learning to live and work as a team was critical not only for their success in the race, but also their survival in one of the most challenging yacht races that exists. Jess went on to successfully lead the team to Hobart and develop her leadership skills. Ironically, she could only enter the race when she turned 18, which meant waiting until 2011, two years after she finished sailing solo around the world. Rules exist everywhere — even for the stars.

Making bold moves

Being a family business, Ella Baché is built around our own values and personality to leverage a unique voice in the marketplace. Ella Baché's advertising has always been bold, and the business has grown around the idea that we push boundaries — that's the personality of the brand and that's what challenger brands do. In 2013 we shot a new brand campaign that was beautiful, contemporary and sophisticated. The shot was of four girls showing healthy skin — no boobs, bottoms or anything that could possibly be deemed as being 'inappropriate'. It was a celebration of confident women in their skin, a position in the market we had always owned and desired. It was exciting to launch the campaign across our stores, billboards, digital and magazines; we had worked hard and crafted something magical.

The morning it went live, I received a phone call from the outdoor Advertising Standards Board to say that the image of the girls not smiling was to be pulled and taken down from all billboards. It was too provocative and sexy and women shouldn't be portrayed like this, but they went on to explain that the image of the girls smiling was okay and could stay. That day snowballed into a storm of controversial media interviews, TV stories and people's opinions. We defended the ad because we had to make sure we had a voice in the market to empower people to feel comfortable in their own skin—after all, we were advertising a healthy skin. I will defend this belief and market position each and every time. The ban was reversed and the campaign went on to be a massive success and win numerous awards. Running a challenger brand and having to punch above your weight against multinationals and public companies means you have to be bold, different and have your voice heard. You can't pay your way to success and there is something really inspiring about that.

Growing up with a dad who had built the brand and marketing alongside Ella and my grandparents by designing creative and innovative marketing campaigns has influenced my approach. I often hear him say, 'don't ask for permission, just apologise later'. Trying to carve out my own voice, growing up in a family business with a legacy to follow, meant being bold. The world is so different now from when my grandparents, or even my father, ran the company, and in many ways there are a lot more rules and regulations around what you can and can't do. I remember some iconic campaigns that my dad developed in the 1990s that really put the brand in the public eye and built its name. Perhaps the most legendary campaign was an ad featuring a group of naked Sydney Swans AFL players, each with a big tube of Ella Baché sunscreen in front of their nether region and the tagline 'Protect Your Largest Organ'. A bold move indeed!

Getting social

Communication and platforms have evolved greatly since the 1990s. Social media and digital platforms now offer consumers a communicative shopfront that enables same-level information and exchange among audiences and the brand creating a long-lasting feedback communication process that gives both the brand and the consumer full-circle engagement. Today it's not only the brand creating perception but also the consumer. This enables — as Seth Godin, a global marketing thought leader, calls it — 'leverage'. All the tools we need to build ourselves are there

Today it's not only the brand creating perception but also the consumer.

for anyone to use. You now have the same access as billion-dollar companies. You can use these tools or not, but you can't deny the access is there. The digital space has seen a fast rise for many indie brands that a decade ago without social media would not have had this opportunity. It also offers an amazing opportunity for brands to share their story with consumers seeking transparency like never before, giving them an understanding of what and who are behind the brands.

A few years ago I read about a well-known nail bar in New York City that had been exposed for paying its staff well below the award wage and leaving them to work in appalling conditions. These conditions were discovered by young millennial New Yorkers, and the story went viral. The following week that business closed down. This shows the power of consumers, transparency and social media today. In the 1980s and 1990s the beauty industry was largely based on traditional and predictable beauty in an aspirational way. The communications model of the past was to create aspiration through imagery, a method that is debated today. Decades ago there was still a high level of conformity within which the beauty and skin industry presented itself. This became an opportunity for Ella Baché's very different brand personality, and the way it expressed itself to the market made us stand out, own our voice and create a space.

In today's digital world, the internet and social media have completely revolutionised the way we communicate and the way we buy things. Our focus today at Ella Baché is getting the attention of our customers where they search, which is Google, Instagram, Facebook, emails and our website. This has created a platform for individuals and brands to amplify their voice in a personalised way that we have never seen before. It also means we operate at breakneck speed. Did you know it took 40 years for 50 million people to get a radio, and it took Facebook just one year to get 50 million followers? We are more connected and networked than ever before. People no longer watch advertisements—when they come on during a TV show, it disrupts what they're watching and annoys them. Most people I know watch Netflix, Stan and other paid networks instead just to avoid ads. The way brands communicate needs to be more relevant and personalised these days. Ads no longer pop up on your TV screen; they visit you on your news feeds and mobiles. The great part about this (for the brands) is that they can now target you more easily. They know where you live, how many kids you have, how much you earn and probably what you had for breakfast. This creates an issue for big global brands as you can no longer simply spend your way to success. Data, understanding your customer and curating relevant and interesting content are key.

I'm guilty of letting my sons use their iPad and I take the view that as long as it's limited and they're outside playing most of the time, it's just what kids today do. But one of their favourite things to watch is Ryan's Toy Reviews on YouTube. At first I had no idea who Ryan was or why they were watching this. After doing five minutes of research, I found out that Ryan—a seven-year-old boy—has the fourth most-watched YouTube channel in the world and is a massive advertising opportunity for brands to reach kids. The need for creativity and owning your voice is greater than ever.

If you can solve people's problems and take to market a great product that has a need, you can leverage social media to get attention pretty effectively.

Similarly, President Trump—like him or hate him—has completely bypassed the media and takes to Twitter, controlling his own messages and what he puts out there. It won him the election. This can either overwhelm you or excite you, or both. Regardless, we live in a digital age and there is no turning back. Starting or running a business today requires great data and speed. I often wonder what the world will be like when my kids are older.

The exciting thing for entrepreneurs is if you can solve people's problems and take to market a great product that has a need, you can leverage social media to get attention pretty effectively.

I was in Singapore in early 2018. It was the week that the first driverless car in LA was launched. I was reflecting on what jobs will be around in the future and what capabilities my kids should be building if so much of what we do becomes automated, making so many jobs redundant. We went to the zoo that day, which is about a 20-minute drive from the centre of Singapore. Looking out of the cab window, I observed that all the 'road workers' were robots: they told us to slow down, pointed out the roadworks and directed us into the zoo. Where a few years ago we would have seen about 30 human road workers along the route of our 20-minute trip, that day there wasn't one in sight. I sat in the back of the cab and wondered if the cab driver was worried about his job since the headlines in all the newspapers that day were about the launch of the first driverless car. Although it's not yet perfected, it's not far away. I came to the conclusion that our kids' creativity and problem-solving abilities need to be nurtured and grown like never before. This leads me to worry about how much the Australian education system is lagging behind other advanced countries.

Finding your voice

As I said earlier, having your own values is essential. You need to find and own your voice, stand for something meaningful, be consistent, and build trust and authenticity to create deep-lasting relationships. In this new digital world content and understanding SEO (search engine optimisation) are king. The best part about this is that it means writing a lot. It means being curious, committed to learning and protecting the creative vision. Where a decade ago it was the big brands that influenced our decisions, as we've already seen, today it's human influencers. People want to know the humans behind the brands: they want to see what's behind the logos and meet the people who created, founded and grew these brands.

Along with owning your voice comes a responsibility to create your personal and professional values with good intentions — to create a voice that's unique to you — and to keep it *simple*. Presenting a clear and consistent message to an entire audience that is universally understood, is the most effective approach. Richard Branson is an expert at this.

A few years ago I went to a work lunch event where I was the only female. I had never met anyone else at the lunch before. The man who was hosting the event said to me, 'When doing your introduction, make sure you say something that will shock people'. I asked him for an example and his response was, 'Just tell everyone that you're a lesbian or something like that'. I was so shocked, I moved away and, although I sat through the event, I couldn't wait to get out of there. This guy was supposedly very successful and ran a well-known company. I couldn't believe he could be so clueless! But I did walk away kicking myself that I didn't stand up and tell him exactly what I was thinking and how wrong his comment was in so many ways. Needless to say, I would never buy from or interact with that company again.

About 12 months before Australia legalised same-sex marriage, I put Ella Baché forward as a brand that supported an LGBT charity. A few weeks later I received a letter from a state politician accusing me and Ella Baché of discriminating against employees who didn't support LGBT equality. It was in that moment that I realised that it's perfectly acceptable to tear up a letter from any well-known person—even a state politician—and throw it in the rubbish bin! We're lucky we live in a country where we can do this, so we have to use our voice and stand up for what we believe in.

I'm often surrounded by strong men in the boardroom or at business-group meetings. Finding a voice and expressing how it is different for women takes speaking out, but in general most men I've come across during my career have been extremely supportive once you get to know them.

So it's great to see this generation is a lot more supportive of women in the workplace and that we've moved forward from when women were each other's worst enemy at work. Unfortunately, I've seen and experienced it all—the jealousy, withholding information, exclusion, competitiveness, cruelty—you name it. I don't believe it's as common for young women these days to feel that they need to struggle, fight and be miserable just because the women before them did.

Practising speaking up

Ella Baché is about being the best you can be and we give many, many women an opportunity to receive a great education and become businesswomen in their own right. I've seen countless girls come out of our Ella Baché College and eventually go on to win awards, build great teams and businesses, and set up an amazing life for themselves. In many cases their partners end up quitting their corporate jobs and working with them in the business. As I've said before, culture is a really important part of Ella Baché and continuing the values that Ella held so close. Celebrating individuality is really important to us, as is ensuring there is zero tolerance for negative behaviour, bitchiness or not supporting your colleagues. Of course we have really healthy debates involving lots of passion, but we also have lots of laughs every day! When it comes to culture and behaviours I use my voice loud and clear if someone is not behaving in a positive way towards someone else. Our great culture comes largely from having so much individuality and diversity in ages, races, tenure and expertise and at the end of the day we embrace that and have a great laugh together, no matter how tough the day has been. I walk into so many different work spaces and offices and the first thing I notice is how quiet they are and that no-one is laughing. Of course you need time to think and work, but business is about people and positive energy—and everyone needs to laugh and smile too!

Owning my voice is something I have had to work on, and still do. I'm certainly not the bossiest, most extroverted person by any means. I've always been very social, so I've always loved getting energy from other people. I've never had any problems with being passionate and putting my ideas forward, but if there is a real bully in the room, that's when I back down as I have a hard time dealing with confrontation. I've had to learn to manage bullies because I'm not a bully naturally, and I've had to learn how to de-power bullies in my life so they don't just override me and own the outcome. I've learned to take a step back and if people have something to say, they need to get it out and feel heard. So

I let people express themselves and in a way it de-powers them a bit—it lets the heat out of the situation. I'll then ask the questions, try to engage them, and try to persuade them and influence them in a very non-threatening way. I never try and out-bully a bully; it won't work.

Finding your voice, stepping out and being visible are uncomfortable. Even though I'm an extrovert, I'm not an off-the-charts extrovert and I do have some shyness about me. I'm not that centre-of-attention person who naturally wants to own that space in the spotlight all the time. Over time, I've learned to be comfortable with owning that visible space and my voice if I'm saying something I'm passionate about and I know I can positively influence the people who are listening. I don't perceive myself to be extraordinary by any means; we're all out there doing our best.

Stepping out of your comfort zone and being visible often opens you to the opinion of others. Being a mum, I'm naturally protective of my kids as they didn't choose the journey that I'm on so ensuring my family remains out of the public eye is very important to me.

Understanding what you want and what you are fighting for certainly means focusing your time and energy and making them a priority. Every day, a hundred different things can erode your focus and energy. Working out what the enablers are to bring your vision or ideal day to life means carving out the time each and every day and deciding how to say *no* to things that aren't going to add value. This is particularly tricky when you have competing things coming at you: work, kids, friends, you name it. Figuring out how best to adapt can really free you up to spend time on the things that mean the most, and that is the topic of chapter 3.

BE BOLD
AND OWN YOUR VOICE

Are you ready to step up and own your voice and your vision?
Here are a few tips.

 ★ Start with clarifying your vision. Get really clear on
   what you want and how you want to feel.

 ★ Be authentic, build trust and hold on to your values.

 ★ When you're passionate about something it's much
   easier to use your voice.

 ★ Speak out if you have a burning desire that needs
   expressing to really make a difference.

 ★ Play to your strengths and differences — we spend
   too much time focusing on trying to improve our
   weaknesses.

 ★ Get social: mass media and generic communication are
   a thing of the past.

 ★ Practice in speaking up builds confidence — sometimes
   you just have to practise again and again.

TALKING BOLD AND OWNING YOUR VOICE
WITH LAYNE BEACHLEY

sat down to interview one of my favourite Aussie women, Layne Beachley.

Layne Beachley AO is regarded as the most successful female surfer in history. Eight times World Champion, she was instrumental in battling to get equal pay for women, which was introduced in 2019 through the World Surf League—a monumental milestone in world sport.

For the past 15 years Layne has, through the Layne Beachley Foundation, provided scholarships to young Australian women.

★ ★ ★

Living a bold life means knowing who you are. By that I mean having a really strong connection with who you are and what you stand for. And then standing up for what you believe in.

To work this out, and what it really means for me, has taken me a lot of reflection, experience and failure. You know, I think about the girl growing up at Manly beach, surfing from the age of four and having that passion for surfing but also the tenacity to continue entering a hostile and threatening environment. Having that clarity of vision around wanting to be the best I can possibly be. And then surrounding myself with the support that's required for me to achieve that vision. So, in saying that, it takes passion, tenacity, vision and support to really show up like that.

I think about all the different times when I've struggled to break through certain challenges or obstacles, and then the skills or the toolbox that I've needed to open up and grab hold of to help push me through those blocks.

I've got a very high risk appetite too, which I consider to be part of living boldly. You know, just like Jess Watson, there are very few women who have sailed solo around the world before their sixteenth birthday, and similarly there are very few women who have surfed 50-foot waves. And there's no other woman who has won six consecutive world titles. Actually, there's no other athlete or surfer who's won six consecutive world titles! So you know you're as bold as your aspirations. I've always had pretty bold aspirations.

All of our beliefs emanate from our childhood. So, if we had a childhood where our main source of inspiration, support and trust came from deliberate knowledge, such as our beliefs that we can do anything and that someone believes in us and demonstrates similar behaviours, then we choose to believe them. But if we have adults in our lives who tell us, 'I believe in you' or 'you're amazing—you can do anything' and then you happen to hear or see them demonstrate behaviour that contradicts that, then you'll believe the behaviour and not the words.

So you have to really be conscious of the role modelling that you play as an adult and also understanding that as children we're narcissists in the first five to seven years of our lives. We're absorbing a lot of information and everything's about us all the time. And

I think about someone like Michelle Payne, for example. Her dad was her biggest fan. Her biggest supporter. He never told her that she couldn't. I think about Gail Kelly: her dad was also her greatest supporter and provider of inspiration and words of encouragement. In the same way, my dad is my greatest supporter. Michelle Payne lost her mum when she was six months old. I lost my mum when I was six years old. So my dad's always been my rock: he's been my source of inspiration, my source of courage.

My dad left school when he was 14. He travelled the world. He became a very successful businessman. And he lived a bold life. I know that the freedom that I had in my childhood — the freedom to run, the freedom to play and most importantly the freedom to fail — is what has given me the tools that I need to live a bold life. I was never scrutinised for my mistakes. I was just able to learn from them as I went. But today I feel that because of the scrutiny and because of social media it's very different for kids. It's creating unrealistic expectations that kids aren't allowed to fail. There's no safety in failure any more, whereas we were fortunate to be brought up in an environment where there was.

We've got this great quote on the back of our bathroom door that basically says congratulations to anyone who was born between the 1930s and the 1970s because that was the generation where we saw an explosion of innovators and risk takers and people who grew up at a time where we were free. If we fell out of trees and broke bones no-one got sued for it. And on a hot day we drank water from a hose. And we shared a coke. We didn't have mobile phones so we actually went over to people's houses and knocked on their doors to ask if they're ready to play ... you know? We played until the street lights were on. There was just so much more freedom. So much more innovation and creativity. If we can bring this back and combine it with the current technical and digital age, it could be really powerful.

The thing that really stops people from living a bold life is fear of failure, fear of consequence, fear of not knowing, fear of looking foolish, fear of screwing up, fear of success. Anything that stops you from stepping into your power and to be innately you is fear. I experienced this when I was competing. I realised that I was my own worst critic because of my fear of being placed on a pedestal, being rejected and being expected to behave in a different way if I became a world champion. I was sabotaging myself. But then the biggest and boldest move I've ever made was retiring from the pro tour of surfing because it meant stepping into the unknown. When I retired from the pro tour I immediately felt this sense of loss, of hopelessness: that I'd lost my identity, my sense of direction, my sense of purpose, my sense of being. It made me realise that my whole sense of self was wrapped up in being a professional surfer. One of the biggest things I learned was that I had to go and recreate a whole new profession, a whole new passion and a whole new avenue to channel my competitive nature. I thought I had to control all that all the time. It wasn't until I realised that it's actually okay to let go that a whole other world opened up to me and I was able to focus my attention on becoming a better speaker and a better presenter, as well as a more loving wife and a more valuable ambassador . . . so yes it was great! I was also able to be a better surfer. I feel like I'm surfing better now than when I was on tour.

I know that the biggest mistake I've made in business is I haven't known what I've wanted. Therefore, I can't ask for what I need.

And if you can't ask for what you need then you don't know who to surround yourself with. So my model for success is all about clarifying your vision. My vision as an athlete was to become world champion. My vision today is actually more centred around how I want to feel versus what I want to achieve. Because if you know how you want to feel that will dictate what actions you take.

The three habits that help me maintain my success and are my model for success are:

- clarifying my vision
- building a dream team
- taking action daily.

I want to feel excited; I don't want to feel drained. I want to feel energised; I don't want to feel restless. And when you know how you want to feel that helps you decide who you surround yourself with. Because there are so many people in our lives who compromise our own values. I call them 'dream thieves' because they suck the life out of you. We all have them in our lives and I used to choose when I allowed them into my space—but I don't any more. Now I choose to only surround myself with quality people to ensure I live a quality life.

I'm hungry and I'm thirsty for knowledge. So, sometimes I will let people know what they don't want to know. I want to shortcut people's pathways, to help people, and I feel the more experiences I share with others, the more they can relate to me—that way they will think, if she is going through it, it can happen to me too.

I have always stood my ground, owned my voice and had a fighting spirit, and when I reflect on the first nine months of my life, I know that what I went through, from being conceived through to being adopted at birth, had a profound effect on the person I've become. My fighting spirit emanates from being thrust into a little crib from the moment I was born — I was six weeks premature, underweight, unhealthy and had to fight for my life. That's been one of my driving forces. And so I've been able to utilise that strength in some of the toughest, most hostile environments.

There have been plenty of times when I've looked back at my story and realised what was holding me back. Whether it was a self-limiting belief, for example, or even growing up in Manly and learning how to surf, feeling so threatened. Lacking support from my male counterparts, I developed this deep underlying belief that men disrespect or don't respect women. Knowing that was preventing me from creating really strong connections with men. Being adopted and having trust issues also held me back and I realised I was being a self-saboteur.

I speak honestly, with transparency, and share my own perspective and experience and it's then up to others to take away from it what relates or pertains to them. I just share honestly through my heart and not from my head. I think the world's crying out for authentic leadership, and that's what I pride myself with offering.

I've had to learn to create boundaries through a clear decision-making process; otherwise I would end up in everyone else's vortex, exhausted and unhealthy. I set my priorities through my vision and ask myself, 'What is it I want to feel?' But as an adoptee, I have a huge fear of rejection so saying *no* is one of my biggest challenges. I had to come up with a way of saying *no* that gave me the confidence to say *no*. If my response is 'hell yeah', I'll jump at it and say 'yes'. Otherwise it's a hard 'no'. Everything in-between, all the should, would, could or doing it out of obligation then becomes a hard *no*. I do everything at 100 per cent, and if I say 'hell yeah', and I can't give 100 per cent of myself to the opportunity, then it's 'no'. If you don't do this, what you're actually doing is you're saying *no* to your health, you're saying *no* to your family, you're saying *no* to the quality relationships that you have—all because you're saying *yes* to everyone and everything. I learned that lesson in the first four years of retirement. I said 'yes' to everyone and everything and ended up with pneumonia.

Another big lesson I learned was that I was really pushy. I had unrealistic expectations of myself and then projected them onto people around me as well. So essentially all I did was keep pushing people away and pushing myself, and it cost me a lot. It cost me a lot of happiness, a lot of joy; it cost me my health and wellbeing. It cost me a lot of friendships, and being pushy and pushing all the time certainly made my ascent to becoming world champion a lot more difficult than it really needed to be and it was totally unsustainable. I look at how much it cost me and I realise that it didn't have to be that hard, but I also had this fundamental belief that success had to be hard and I believe a percentage of the population agree that if we don't work really hard and flog ourselves to death then it's not worth it and we don't deserve it. So, I've learned to trust in something different and that's called 'ease and grace'. And I've proven that that can be a successful model by winning my seventh and eighth full titles.

Ease, grace and gratitude, and grounding yourself in an attitude of gratitude on a daily basis, centres you and brings you back to that state. So I refer to my pushy side as my survival mode mechanism and I know that when I'm in that mode I'm in a state of pain: it's hard, it's a struggle — you almost feel the weight of it. And when I go to ease and grace it lightens me up and I become more trusting; it becomes more effortless and an opportunity to open up anew.

I want to feel excited and elated and energised when I wake up every day, and if I'm not then that vision becomes my accountability, and I ask myself, 'Why am I not feeling energised and excited today?' Did I drink too much? Did I party too hard? Am I working too hard? Am I compromising my sleep? Am I travelling too much? Am my saying 'yes' to things and it's not a 'hell yeah'? That becomes my accountability partner. So get really clear on how it is that you want to feel because that will determine what you want and what decisions you make after that.

And then, finally, build yourself up with a team of people that hold you accountable and also support you.

Chapter 3
DESIGN YOUR LIFE

Some are born great, some achieve greatness,
and some have greatness thrust upon them.
William Shakespeare

How do you go beyond what's expected and start making your own rules and decisions so that you design your own life?

Be willing to adapt

Wife … mother … running a big business … sitting on boards … and making time for friends and exercise. One of the questions I often get asked is, 'How do you do it all?' The answer is because I *don't* do it all. Michael, my husband, shares the load equally with me. We choose to do it this way and it works for us (well, most of the time anyway). We choose to set our rhythm this way and design our lives so we can share parenthood equally. We made the decision that we would both work, but we always make sure one of us is home each day at 5 pm. So if we travel, we travel separately and we often attend evening events alone. (I often think people don't believe I have a husband because I'm so often out on my own.) We also choose to have a wonderful nanny, Issy, a few days a week (I don't like using the word 'nanny' as she's part of our family). She brings so much value to our lives. We too share the work at home and in the office: she's amazing. She's 25, considers herself a working mum and contributes equally. We all accept our own strengths and weaknesses and share the belief that life is lived through playing to your own strengths. The kids are happy, healthy and have a great life full of love from lots of people.

Having two boys, it's important for me that they learn from a young age to respect women and embrace strong women. I want them to understand that men and women are to be celebrated equally. By appreciating women I hope they will grow into confident, independent, happy men who respect themselves, but equally respect women. Too many women I've worked with in the past burned out and fell apart because they were trying to do it all: the full-time worker, the mum who is there to drop off or pick up her kids and everything in between. Their partners don't help out much at home or with the kids and it becomes too much for one person to manage alone. Women aren't great at asking for help, but responsibilities need to be shared.

One of the best pieces of advice I received when I first had kids while I was running the business was 'you just have to keep adjusting'. And it's true: some days your kids need you more and some days the business does. There's no hard and fast rule. Every day is different. The daily juggle is certainly not for the faint-hearted. When my first son, Lachie, was born, I attempted to take maternity leave, but it didn't play out that way. The business needed me too, so after about a month I juggled the two. Many days I found myself at home on my work computer with a newborn on my chest, my eyes popping out of my head with tiredness. That was really, really hard and the one emotion I have had to avoid buying into is guilt. Someone once said to me 'guilt is a wasted emotion' and one I know all mums suffer from. Whether you're working full time or staying at home, there's always going to be guilt lingering in some form and I have had to be disciplined around cutting it off and not feeding the emotion. It's a really hard thing to do, and I struggle every day with this conflict. I want to be at work, but I also want to be with the kids. I remind myself that just because I work, it doesn't mean that I'm not present and hands-on in their daily lives. There's a saying: 'if you want something done, give it to a busy person'. I'm that busy person and I often feel shattered by the end of the day, but it's amazing how resilient we are and how much we can get done if we have to. You have to do your best and own your responsibilities.

Lachie was one of those babies who only settled sleeping on my chest. Before I had him everyone said to me, 'don't worry — babies just sleep for the first few months. It's like their fourth trimester'. Bloody hell — that wasn't our experience. This kid nearly broke us! He was born with his eyes open and never slept in a cot. I spent many hours, days and nights with a newborn on my chest, laptop on the floor and mobile under my chin. I used to pump a bottle of milk in the mornings so my husband could do the 4 am feed when Lachie woke up just so I could get an extra hour's sleep.

Someone once said to me 'guilt is a wasted emotion'.

One day, I knew I had pushed my multitasking too far when I was on a conference call, pumping milk (if you don't know what that sounds like, think of a cow milking machine) and the poor person on the other end of the phone asked me, 'What is that noise?' I couldn't bring myself to tell them, so I replied 'What noise?' Mums out there, I know you can agree with me on this one: just when you think you have a routine going with kids, they throw a spanner in the works and change it all. My best advice is to adapt and go with it. I didn't have the luxury of sleeping when my babies slept; instead, they went straight into the pram and I would pound the pavement while taking my daily phone calls.

For me it's important to be clear on my values. A decision I've owned since day one is that I wanted a family and I wanted a career. It hasn't been easy, but the network I created around me made it a journey with learning along the way. I would never turn up at work and complain about how tired I was. It wasn't anyone else's fault and we all have stuff going on in our private lives. So I put on a smile, had another coffee and made the most of the day.

I would often turn up to my mother's group after a board meeting or conference call, my mind in the depths of the business. I would find myself sitting in a conversation focused on the best place to buy nappies. This was a jolt for me—I would even at times find myself being envious of having the space to think about such things. That wasn't my story. Instead, I wonder if my kids will know about formulating products, managing the supply chain, developing strategies and reading P&Ls by the time they are 10! The other day, Lachie wanted me to jump on the trampoline with him and he turned to me and said, 'Come on, Mum. Just use your strategies!'

Today women, especially mums, get pulled in all directions, giving to everyone with nothing left for themselves, and somewhere along the line it has turned into a social norm that we're expected to hold down a career, raise a well-adjusted family, have a social life, save the world and not forget an annual holiday that represents something out of a traveller's magazine. For me, not all of this was going to be possible. With kids came exhaustion and I may have sometimes found myself sitting in a boardroom with a shirt on inside out and back to front. Thankfully men don't tend to notice these things. Looking back, there are many days and weeks that I don't even remember. The sleep deprivation was real, but I was determined to have a seat at the table and wasn't going to let a baby make me give up that seat. That was my choice — not his.

Having young children made me feel like I needed to give up the things that I used to do to re-fuel myself: a massage, a yoga class. It seemed obvious that I had to give these up because time was limited now and I was permanently sleep deprived. It took me a good year after having my first baby to realise that it was the yoga class, the massage or the 15-minute jog that gave me the energy I needed to keep giving. By the time baby number two came along, I became determined to give myself permission to do things for myself. So I went to the gym on the way home from work every day and jumped onto the treadmill and bike for 20 minutes to get those endorphins going. It gave me the energy to walk through my front door and be available to my kids, rather than wanting to fall on the floor. Sunday yoga classes and monthly massages made the world of difference too!

Learning to say *no*

I've always been focused. My husband regularly comments on how I have the ability to block everything out and stay focused on what I'm doing. One of my roles is to not panic when others do; I think most CEOs get used to this. Your tolerance for disasters slowly increases, allowing you to have energy for when a real disaster comes along.

The thing that rattles me the most is when I haven't protected my space and rhythm of the day. When I pack too much into the diary and when everyone needs a piece of me and I should have said 'no' more often instead of 'yes'. It's my constant learning to check if saying 'yes' to things is going to set the day and myself up to fail. It's one of the hardest lessons to learn when you are a *yes* person and a doer! But I've learned to say 'no'. So now, on many occasions when people walk into my office and ask, 'Have you got 5 minutes?' I say, 'No, sorry, not now', and go back to them when I have some space. I've become much better at making no apologies for doing this because the alternative is much worse for me, the business and them.

I've also become a lot better at backing my decisions based on my experience, as my biggest mistakes happen when I haven't listened to my instinct. As Ella Baché offers a franchise model, people regularly come to us enquiring about opening a salon. It's so important who you get into a partnership with and who you let into the network. In some cases, it's a 15-year relationship and in many cases it's a lifetime. Life's too short to work with people whose heart is not in the right place.

I once had to turn down a lady who was very keen to open a business. She had just come into some money and wanted something to do. She was a customer of the brand, but she wasn't up for the commitment you need to run the business and look after staff and customers. So we agreed that she would go and work in one of our salons to get a feel for it. This salon was a well-performing business with a great owner I had a close relationship with. The interested lady reported back after her experience with all the things the owner should be doing differently. I knew she would never be the right fit and we decided it was best to go our separate ways. A week later I went to the snow and the lodge I was staying at held a dinner for its members. It just so happened that she was sitting at the dinner table. That was awkward, to say the least!

Life's too short to work with people whose heart is not in the right place.

I've learned that so many people are willing to point out your flaws or the flaws of others, especially when you're a leader. I often hear, 'That idea won't work; we don't like how that looks' and so on. Surround yourself with people who push you forward and give you momentum and if they don't, it's okay to go your separate ways—sometimes for the short term and sometimes forever. This makes space in your life for the right people to come in.

Protecting your space

I'm conscious that I've spent a lot of my life taking action and moving forward. It can mean I miss out on some moments, especially ones with the kids. My dad calls it the 'can't stop club'. It's true, but it's just because there are so many great things to experience—including having kids—and I don't want to miss out. I was even curious to see if my view of the world would change when I had kids.

I've always been a worker—a hard worker. It's in my DNA. Growing up around a family business, you don't know any differently when you're a kid. But I think back to what I was exposed to and it definitely shaped my work ethic, focus, drive and love of work. I think back to my great-aunt Ella and my grandparents, who lived through some of the most disruptive times in history—experiencing war and living through the Great Depression—yet still they went on and created new lives in foreign countries, prepared to work for anything. They were forced to be inventive and bold. They had no networks, no family and no certainty. It was also an era without Facebook or any digital communication platforms so they worked hard to make friends, create networks and turn their passions into a reality through hard work and conviction. They had to back themselves and fortunately never felt like they had to pretend to be anyone else.

I've never believed in work–life balance. There are no strict dividing lines or 'on' and 'off' switches. It's a choice of how you want to live your life. And with technology you're 'on' all the time anyway.

Having kids has made me more hard core about protecting my space. I used to be the first one in the office and the last one out: set examples … work the longest and the hardest … These days, although I'm often the first one in (as it gives me the space to organise myself, think and do what I need to do), I'm a lot more outcome focused than time focused, and I can happily say I am no longer always the last one out. I'm impatient with people who set wasteful meetings, turn up unprepared or waffle on. Time is the most precious commodity, so don't waste it, especially when it's not yours to waste.

My kids have taught me to put rules around people, break the co-dependencies and set my own space. If I'm not of value at work, then I should be with my kids.

I make a conscious decision to create relationships with people who bring me happiness and positivity. Once your kids reach school age, a whole new world opens up for you, including being around other mums. They can be so tough on each other and so judgemental and competitive. I choose to never buy into this. A few years ago I was at a kids' play date with some mums and their children. One mum came up to me and asked, 'What's it like to have someone else raise your kids?' I was floored because I couldn't believe I'd heard such a loaded question from someone I'd never even met before. But it gave me a massive insight into this world of mums—it was like going back to school—and I realised I needed to make a deliberate decision about who I have in my space and who I don't.

Own the rhythm of your life

I was lucky to have great parents. They never put any specific pressure on me to join Ella Baché, even though I knew the ins and outs from an early age and spent hours and days there and at home listening to them talk about the business. There was never an expectation to join the family business, but there was definitely an expectation to be passionate about whatever I did, give it my all, work hard and go way beyond what was required. Many were silent expectations that played out in more complex ways. Being thrown in the deep end just became the norm and what was expected. Sink or swim. Many times it would have been amazing to have some support, but my family's view was always 'this is your experience—I can't do it for you so you're on your own'. Hard…tough…too much responsibility…but you certainly learn to survive.

After I finished school I remember thinking I just wanted to be a free spirit and have my own adventures—my own experiences. I left home when I was 18 and moved into a shared house with friends while we were at uni and working. It was chaos—never any food, and everything in disorder—but I craved it. After finishing uni, I wanted to get as far away as possible from my parents, not because I didn't love them but because I needed my own adventure. I moved to London and again lived in a shared house, slightly more chaotic than the first, but again exactly what I craved. I was always filled with wanderlust, and had the desire to travel the world, explore new places, meet new people and discover new things. I'm still filled with this desire and any time I feel 'stuck' I know freedom is only a plane trip away.

Today I have the challenge of instilling my work ethic and values into my kids, Lachie and Darcy, and making sure they can make the right bold decisions in their lives. I recently went to a seminar called 'Raising gorgeous boys' (I'm sure there are similar seminars for raising girls). What shocked me about boys was hearing that they are four times as likely to die between the ages of 14 to 25 years and 19 times more likely to go to prison, so keeping boys alive and protected from motor vehicle accidents, violence and mental health illnesses is an enormous task for parents and society. Maggie Dent and Steve Biddulph spoke at the one-day event and provided some good tips to help parents ensure boys make the right decisions in life including how to create family values together so your kids can choose right from wrong. They suggest that your kids understand and live by three rules. First, don't hurt yourself; second, don't hurt others; and third, don't hurt the world around you. We don't have the luxury of a village to raise our kids, and like us our kids need good role models. After all, a role model is someone you should try to emulate.

I was fortunate to have grown up in a family that included friends who were fantastic role models and I know that role models certainly don't have to be your blood family. Boys need to know what it is to be a good man and move from childhood to manhood. The message about promoting manhood that I walked away with from the seminar was *being able to stand in your own emotions and not let them spill over to hurt yourself or anyone around you.* I love this. It's our role to do our best to create good little humans, no matter what the gender, while moving from childhood to adulthood. Parenting is the hardest and best job in the world. Another tip I got from the seminar that I'd like to share was to write a letter to your child every year and point out all the good things they have done that make them a great human. But make sure you make a copy of the letter, so when they are 15 years old and rip it up you have a copy that you can give them later in life.

Travelling helped me discover the meaning of synchronicity. Carl Jung discovered it, and many others, such as Deepak Chopra, still talk about it today. The term they use is 'flow'. When you get in the right rhythm and flow, that's when the magic happens—when opportunities open up and meaningful coincidences come your way. It's much easier to get into the 'flow' when you're travelling and have the time and space to remain open. The challenge is to keep this flow going when life is more structured, routined and disciplined. There is an element of luck in everyone's success, but luck comes and goes. It's your ability to identify those moments that determine success. You won't be successful if you focus on your weaknesses—which most of us naturally spend 80 per cent of our time focusing on. We need to flip our thinking and focus on our strengths. I talk more about this in chapter 6.

> When you get in the right rhythm and flow, that's when the magic happens—when opportunities open up and meaningful coincidences come your way.

It was from moving away and discovering myself and what I wanted along the way that I began to own the rhythm of my life—in other words, working out what I wanted and how I was going to get it.

Setting boundaries

As a CEO and a mum, I've had to learn to be firm and set boundaries, otherwise I just end up being exhausted. I've learned that you have to be consistent with the boundaries you set and the messages you send to others and—as I've already stressed—you need to be okay with saying 'no'. The best days are when I hold the boundaries firmly and focus on the priorities and what needs doing. I made a rule when I had children that I was going to work four days a week until my kids went to school. That way I'd have one day a week to spend with them one-on-one. That was really important to me. It doesn't mean that I work any less; it's about working smarter and being there when people need you the most. It was an interesting learning because it probably took a few months for people to realise I wasn't in the office on a Friday, but it empowered them to make decisions on their own, and to really step up, which wouldn't have happened as much if I was there. I had unconsciously created co-dependency, where I would go around solving everyone's problems, and it didn't do me or them any favours. The same applies to my kids: I have to stop myself jumping in and doing things for them, and instead support them to do things by themselves.

I have learned to become a lot better at planning and designing my life, which has meant I am clear on my priorities and the things I say 'yes' to. I've also become much better at saying 'no' to the things and people that don't excite me or add any value to my life. While there are times when I need to be spontaneous, try new things and have new adventures, I find my weeks are best when they are carefully planned. Each week is different, and what works one week doesn't always work for another, so I just keep moving forward and adjusting as I go. There is no perfect balance and when you want to live a bold life I have learned it's often all or nothing. I just need to take the time out to breathe and reflect occasionally!

BE BOLD
AND DESIGN YOUR LIFE

You have to own your rules, go beyond what's expected and defend your decisions. Here are a few tips.

* Back yourself and find your voice.
* Keep adjusting your life to make it work for you.
* Your tolerance for dealing with disasters slowly increases with experience so you can manage the real disaster when it comes.
* Be clear on your values because they become a guide for the decisions you make.
* Figure out where you are going to make the greatest impact and spend time doing that.
* Give yourself permission to say 'no' to things that don't excite you or work for you.
* Own 'no' gracefully, without over-compensating.
* Protect your space.
* Surround yourself with people who push you forwards and give you momentum.
* Set boundaries and rules and don't be swayed by others.
* Be consistent with your messages—there's nothing worse than flip-flopping.
* Find out what you want out of life—what you stand for—and own your rhythm.

TALKING BOLD AND DESIGNING YOUR LIFE
WITH CAROLYN CRESWELL

I sat down with Carolyn Creswell, who 25 years ago took a part-time job helping make muesli once a week while she studied at uni. Carolyn made a bid for the business when it went up for sale to ensure she could keep her part-time job. At the time she had no idea how big it would become 25 years later.

Today Carolyn runs a multimillion-dollar business, Carman's Muesli; is a mum of four; an amazing Australian entrepreneur; and an ambassador and board member to human rights organisations. Carolyn inspires me with the way she designs her life around the rhythm and speed that she wants, and by going beyond what's expected and making her own rules. With an incredible sense of perspective, and a pragmatic approach, Carolyn creates boundaries, rules and structures along the way, which has enabled her to learn who she is, what she wants and what she is comfortable with. This has meant learning to say 'no' gracefully.

★ ★ ★

It takes a long time to feel comfortable in your own skin and to know what you enjoy doing; to really get in touch with who you are, and what motivates you. To discover your purpose and what motivates you every day to want to go and do what you're doing. Initially, I probably worried too much about what other people thought and I was very much a yes-yes-yes person. I am now able to really selectively do things that I feel enrich my life and make me feel better: that I'm making a difference, and that I'm enjoying the journey. It's taken a fair bit of time to sort and navigate through everything. I was someone who was always running late for a plane. I thought the definition of success was always being really busy and if you asked me how I was, I'd say I was so busy, constantly running from here to there. You know, working nights, working weekends — and I thought that meant I'd made it. It wasn't sustainable.

I'm bold, but still I'm a calm person. I still have time for my friends; I've got four kids under the age of 14; I work full-time, but I'm a great mum. I'm terrible at lots of other things, trust me. But I still feel that you are constantly challenging yourself, and looking at further opportunities. You're not just letting yourself get complacent. Some people live a small life, which can become a little bit too gossipy. I love Eleanor Franklin's quote about small minds discussing people and great minds discussing ideas. I ask myself, 'How can we make the world a better place?' Let's have much more interesting conversations, rather than 'Did you see what she wore to that party on Saturday night?'

People can get a little bit obsessed with keeping up with the Joneses. So you can end up living in a bubble, then before you know it everything becomes the norm. I look at some of the mums I know from school, and it's just endless rounds of coffee mornings and going to the gym and whatever. I want to say to them that they should get out of this suburb, and go and volunteer one morning for the Asylum Seeker Resource Centre. Or go and do something where you see people who have a lot less than you and gain some perspective.

The first thing I do when I have a big day ahead and things get overwhelming is tip my whole handbag out on a desk, or my table, and get really organised. It's my ground-zero. I sort out my bag and take the receipts out of my wallet. And then I'll grab a bit of paper and write down the people I need to call or a few things I need. I just get a little bit of order and then I can attack the day a bit better and get on top of it.

We can all churn through an enormous amount of work and sometimes it's creating that space to go. I can get a lot of work done in a café — probably twice as much as I could if people who know me are around. So sometimes I'll go down to the café and just pump it out — and I won't leave until my inbox is empty.

I went to a place called Gwinganna. It's a health farm in Queensland, a really fantastic place, and they taught me that sometimes the stress I was putting my body under was crippling me. Then I realised that this wasn't the life I wanted to lead and I really needed to adjust a lot of things. I needed to learn to say 'no' a lot more and I've become much better at that. I needed to be able to ask myself, what are the things that I want to commit to and to be prepared to say I'm going to put time into. I'd get asked to be on lots of boards but then I'd rush there and I hadn't read the board papers and I'd felt guilty. So I decided, who am I trying to impress by being on all these different boards? I needed to pull it back, lead a little bit of a simpler life, do less, enjoy it more and try to just take away a lot of the stress.

I try and keep it real. We all have bad days and we probably don't run to social media to tell people about them, but I try not to put myself in situations that I know are not going to make me feel good. I'm always about self-reflection. I just really try to be selective of how I spend my time and what I say 'yes' to. Even if it's what I choose to wear. If I'm having to adjust my clothes all day or hoick my stockings up or whatever, I know that's not a day where I'm going to feel good. So I'll put on my boots and feel my awesome, comfy self and know I'm going to be happy.

Living a bold life is living a big life. It's living your dream life and I'm really conscious of what the things are that I would like to be able to do and what I am working towards, recognising amazing experiences and grabbing opportunities. And so it's just living that full, rich life and that's not necessarily about being a workaholic and thinking 'one day I'm going to get there'. Enjoying the journey and loving what you do and having fun and making the right choices for humanity, and best of all laughing until your stomach muscles hurt, is what it's about.

I learned that my natural style is to seek a bit too much approval; I like everyone to like me and sometimes you have to understand that not everyone's going to like you and you're going to rub some people up the wrong way or whatever and you have to accept that. That doesn't come to me naturally. But then you just have to be a bit of Teflon and shake that off a bit: learning it's okay to do what you need to do, getting on with it and moving on.

My morning routine, my rituals and how I stick to them are important. I will get up and start the day with hot water and lemon juice. Then I meet my girlfriend at 6.15 am and we'll walk the park for an hour and chat, which covers off a lot of things. It offers a sense of being able to chew the fat and work through issues but also exercise and be in nature and I think that's a really great way to start my day. There's a really good book by Tim Ferriss called *Tools of Titans,* which goes through some very interesting people's morning routines. It's how I build refection into my life.

I always take January off and I spend a couple of weeks thinking back to the year that's been and deciding what I'd like to change and what I could do differently in my day. I remember the first year I did this I started small: 'I'm going to floss my teeth every day, and wash my face at night'. As it's progressed I've added more things. Last year I decided I want to see my parents more but I needed to embed this into my life's cycle. I would invite my mum and dad and my husband's mum every Monday night at 6 o'clock for dinner. So you embed these little changes so that when you get to the end of the year, they're just things that have become part of your routine. I enjoy a sense of reflection by writing it up. That way, I can check, 'Have I done it? How am I tracking on this?' That makes me feel good. So you want be thinking about your day and what's important.

One thing I'm really conscious of is 'What's in this for me?' And I know that sounds selfish but realistically everyone's trying to find what's in it for them. I've had to learn to say 'no' gracefully. Greg McKeown's book *How to Say No Gracefully* talks about acknowledging relationships. For example, 'I love seeing your name pop into my inbox…unfortunately I can't mentor your cousin, or have a coffee with your cousin next week to talk about his career…however, what I can do is talk to your cousin when I've dropped the kids off at school…I'm happy to ring your cousin any morning at 9 o'clock'. So I know every morning while I'm driving after school drop-off I have some time in transit to help someone out, which works for me as it's dead time. It's being nice about it but also being firm. You can't say *yes* to everything because time is the one resource that definitely runs out every day. So make sure you protect it and live the life you want to live!

I think if you're living in a little world where all you're trying to do is be the same as everyone else, that's not necessarily finding your journey, your purpose or your interests. You don't go to art galleries just because you feel it's the cool thing to do. If you love art, fantastic, but if you don't, it's totally fine to want to spend the afternoon cooking an amazing meal.

For me it's about reaching your potential. So what is potential? What's the potential of you and your health, for instance? Eating healthily and taking care of yourself. Wearing too much makeup instead of walking out the door with no makeup on and feeling good.

The boldest thing I could do is run around my office and cuddle everyone and say 'thank you', showing gratitude and appreciation. Some people aren't so good with public displays of affection, but you know what, that's my thing.

Chapter 4

STEP INTO YOUR POWER

The problem isn't aiming too high and missing;
it's not aiming high enough.
Unknown

What stops you from pushing through moments of self-doubt?

There's a fine line between taking on a lot and being motivated by it and taking on too much and being overwhelmed by it. I love what I do at work and I love being a mum, so I'm really passionate about both my work and family, which is my driving force. But of course I get overwhelmed and when I do I just compartmentalise it: I break it down and just take one day at a time, sometimes one hour at a time. No-one trains for a marathon by starting with 40 kilometres. I don't run marathons (in fact, I don't run—I'm hopeless at it). But if I did,

I would run 1 kilometre and build up every day from there. It's no different from anything else in your life. And every day is different — that's what I love.

Self-doubt can make you feel vulnerable, and being vulnerable is hard. I'm an open person and I can easily share my mistakes and be vulnerable, especially with people who are on the same journey as me. (Humour always helps too.) But there's a limit to who I'll share my mistakes with: if I feel like I'm being judged, or if people are going to use it against me, I won't open up. But I can also easily take the piss out of myself!

I will naturally stand up and tell people, 'We shouldn't have done this'. Being apologetic isn't hard for me. In fact, I'll say, 'You know what? It was a deliberate decision. I made a mistake'. In life, in business, you fail — but you have to try, you have to innovate. And if you don't, you kind of go backwards. So that's the way I do it. Everyone makes mistakes — it's how you learn from them that matters.

Astro Teller is an outstanding scientist and entrepreneur who works for Google directing its Google X laboratories. He heads a team of engineers and scientists. The hardest thing is getting

Everyone makes mistakes — it's how you learn from them that matters.

them to let an idea go when it's dead or not going anywhere. So, once a year, on the same day every year, they have a ritual where everybody gets together and lets their ideas die. They celebrate having had all of the ideas they've been working on that are just not going to go anywhere and they burn them. In other words, they celebrate their failures. Then they start the next day with a fresh page.

Getting over self-doubt

As women, we're pretty good at admitting our mistakes. I've found what holds a lot of women back is that they worry about the mistakes they *might* make. Fear stops them from making bold moves. We're less likely to take a risk than men in most cases.

What I think is harder to do—and I believe is a part of living a bold life—is talking about your wins. Talking about your successes. Talking about the things that you are good at. Like putting yourself out there as an expert at something or as someone who has achieved something. Is that something that you've naturally been good at or something that you've had to work really hard on? I think we are so ingrained as women to not have a big ego or self-promote that it's easier to let things go unnoticed and just fit in and be part of the crowd. It's the same as reaching out and asking a question. It's amazing the times I have done that. Even writing this book and asking women to contribute and be interviewed for it—I was blown away how easy it was and how everyone just said 'yes'!

Finding your voice and expressing your ideas, especially at a boardroom table, can be hard if you let yourself slip back into that role of the little girl who is meant to sit there, facilitate the conversation, and make sure everyone is okay, no-one feels hurt and everyone is heard instead of stepping forward and putting your opinion on the table.

I'm really conscious of it, and still today, after years of experience, I find myself getting sucked back into that role. Changing your old habits and patterns is really hard to do. If there are areas where I get stuck—mainly self-promotion, and pushing myself out there, which I like to do in a natural way so that it feels good—then I'll try to collaborate with other people to overcome this. I love the collaborative process. It's more fun working something out with someone else; you get to talk through ideas and moments of doubt. No-one ever has all the answers.

If I am really passionate about something I will speak my mind and fight for it. Fighting for something is a good thing as it gives you more 'fire in the belly' when people say no. I have always been a fighter when I believed in something. My mum used to say to my husband, Michael, 'You will never win against Pippa; she will keep going and going until she is blue in the face'. When I was a baby I used to hold my breath if I didn't get my own way, so my mum took me to the doctor and asked for his advice. He said, 'It's not your daughter's problem, it's actually yours!' Turns out being determined is in my blood—sorry Mum!

It's one thing to be bold when you've got all the energy in the world, you've had the sleep you need and you're feeling 100 per cent. It's another thing to conquer self-doubt or make bold moves when you haven't. There's always something going on: you're sick, someone else is sick, you have young children … Some days the energy just isn't there. We're only human. We can't live our best, boldest game-face self every day. On the days when I have no choice but to step out and do things boldly, I do what I need to do and no more. Sometimes that means limiting myself to an hour of being on, with two coffees down.

Following your dreams

It was 2009, and I had just stepped into the role of CEO at Ella Baché when I met Jessica Watson for the first time. She was looking for sponsors to support her in her vision of sailing solo around the world. It struck me that Jess was no ordinary 16-year-old girl. She was gutsy, pioneering, focused and extraordinary. She had done her homework and pulled the right team of experts around her, so we decided she deserved to be backed in pursuing her dream. The number of phone calls I took from the media around the decision to support Jess was hard core. On more than one occasion I quietly questioned the decision and then quickly shrugged off my doubts because intuitively I knew she was amazing and about to do great things. I really had no choice: she is what we're about as a family, a brand and a nation. Jess was a great fit and I had no problem defending her.

Jess left Sydney Harbour in October 2009. I was there with a handful of people, including her parents, to wave Jess good-bye—and off she went in her boat *Ella's Pink Lady*. It was the size of a toenail but had become a safe and reliable friend to Jess. For the next seven months, Jess would call intermittently to check in and update us on how she was going. She was unassuming, respectful and brave, and I had enormous respect for her, even at that age.

The next time I saw Jess was when she sailed back into Sydney Harbour. I still get goosebumps thinking about that day. It was May 2010; we were on a boat in Sydney Harbour waiting anxiously for Jess to appear on *Ella's Pink Lady*. The swell was big, and just sitting out there waiting for her to sail through the heads was enough for me—how she did it for seven months I have no idea. The whole nation stopped to welcome Jess back in—you couldn't move in the harbour with all the boats, sirens, television crews and cameras. Where was everyone before she left? Why had everyone forgotten about the firestorm of controversy?

Why did everyone support her now and not a year ago? There had been much criticism, especially from the politicians and media. How would Jess be feeling? An introvert who had spent the past seven months on her own, only 16 years old, now stepping off the boat to face all these people, including Kevin Rudd, the then prime minister of Australia? Sailing into a storm of publicity and sponsorship deals, Jess took it all in her stride—respectful, intelligent, older and wise beyond her years—and from that day, she became a hero. For my part, I was proud to have backed her as she rightly deserved. It was extraordinary.

In business and in life you need to be brave, take risks and follow your heart.

In business and in life you need to be brave, take risks and follow your heart; otherwise you'll never get anywhere. It takes a certain passion and desire to do something that's great enough that it becomes all-consuming. You need to follow your dreams and not your fears. How big are your dreams? Are they as big as they can be? I had an opportunity to talk to Jess and discover what the real driving force behind her amazing feat was. You'll find her story on page 95.

Embracing change

So many women around me suffer from that all-too-familiar feeling of self-doubt and lack of confidence and I find myself questioning how more women could own their power, their potential. It's certainly normal—I would even say common—to feel self-doubt. I liken it to self-sabotage: in love, health and when going for opportunities and dreams. Self-doubt can haunt you for years until you get to the 'enough' stage—until that day when you wake up and you've had enough of feeling that way. Reaching the 'enough' stage becomes a crucial part in your development. It forces change, and it forces *you* to change. One of my all-time heroes, Sir Richard Branson, once said, 'We can all create our own luck by taking the necessary risks to open the door to change'. As I said earlier, I've found the best way to overcome a lack of confidence is to collaborate on a project with someone else.

It really is about the journey. I didn't always perceive myself as the world did. I felt like I didn't own the title of CEO (titles don't mean much to me). I was Ella's niece and a third-generation CEO in the family business. I had to prove myself not only in everyone else's mind but especially in my own. I didn't have a job description and I certainly didn't have a rule book. I remember sitting at my desk in the first few weeks of becoming CEO and thinking, 'What now? What am I supposed to be doing? What does success look like? And how do I get there?' The thing about being a CEO is that you're supposed to know everything, right? I decided to just work hard. I learned every aspect of the business. I learned it at 30 000 feet and at 3 feet. I believe that set me up to succeed today. I got in the detail, I got my hands dirty and I would never ask someone to do something that I wasn't willing to do myself. Today, I don't need to be in the office all the time. Technology allows you to work from anywhere at any time, which is fantastic for mums. I work at all hours from all places around the kids. As long as the outcomes are achieved, I'm not attached to how people, including myself, achieve them.

I remember, in my early days of being a CEO, being invited to charity events in Sydney. I was surrounded by CEOs from many well-known Australian companies. The difference between me and them was that I was, on average, 20 years younger than everyone else, and that I was female. I viewed it as a social experiment after a while and had fun with it. I saw the humour in it. I certainly became okay with being the odd one out. But I rocked up time and time again, and like everything, once you're comfortable with who you are, others become comfortable with you too. You have to fake it until you make it. You don't earn the right to do something until you've done it—and it takes confidence to do it.

Having kids changed my view on work and business. It didn't dampen my desire or motivation, it just changed things. I had arranged a company event on the same day as my older son's first birthday. Without even thinking about the date I locked it in six months prior to the event. A month out it dawned on me: how could I double book my own son's first birthday? What sort of mother does that! I couldn't change it as it would have meant changing the plans of more than 100 people, as well as guest speakers, venues and so on. I felt so torn—like the worst mum in the world—for not being there for Lachie's birthday. Then one of my best friends said to me, 'Don't worry—just celebrate it the next day. At that age kids don't know what date it is, so just pretend it's the next day. He will never know'. She was right! We had a great first birthday for him, and celebrated the following day without having to move the company conference! Luckily kids give you about three years' grace before they are old enough to realise your slippages and hold you to account. Your definition of success changes when you become a mum. Life gets much better and much broader. But there are also trade-offs and sacrifices. Working only four days in the office has allowed me the flexibility to spend quality time with the kids, and be part of their kindy and schooling. But I'm certainly not the mum who volunteers for everything. I try and do my part and it's wonderful to learn what I'm meant to be doing as a kindy or school mum and to play a role in their ever-changing life.

I try to be and am supportive of and sensitive to other mums. It's the hardest job in the world and they need support, not criticism. I remember when I first had Lachie, my dad said to me, 'If you find mums are telling you that their baby is easy and doing everything right, they are lying!' It was such good advice, especially on those days when I felt I was walking around in circles and hadn't achieved anything, or everything I tried to do didn't work!

Getting digital

Over the past few years, we have had to redesign the business, leverage new opportunities and let go of some of the old ways of doing things. This is because our customers have changed: the way they communicate, the way they buy, the way they want to interact with us and what influences them has all changed. It's not easy when you believe in something and everyone tells you it can't be done—but you have to hold strong and back yourself. I try and look past the 'noise' for real signals and trends. That's why data is invaluable—it takes the emotion out of the situation.

In 2017 we completely changed the way we operated our business. I strongly believed we had to. Our customers had changed and our competition had changed so we too needed to change. I could see this as a consumer myself—what I wanted and what I didn't want any more—when doing business with different companies and brands. So we went to the drawing board and re-designed the way we communicated, and how we treated the skin and other parts of the business. It created a lot of fear, a lot of change, but I had to hold strong as I could see the bigger picture and where things were going. I become obsessive about finding better ways of doing things. I was focused and motivated because I wanted to prove that it could be done, despite some opposition to the ideas. Sometimes I sit on the couch at night for hours and look at the different ways people book services online in our industry and others. I need to understand the detail to then build and re-design the bigger picture around putting myself in our customers' shoes.

This is not only the case in the beauty industry. When was the last time you did your banking at a bank or booked a flight in a travel agent's office? Technology has changed the way we do things and it's a great reminder that nothing stays the same in life or in business. And really, why would you want it to? So we explore, trial new things—sometimes they work, sometimes they don't—and we keep moving forward. Could there be a better way, a smarter way? Sometimes breaking old ways of doing things is the only way to invent, reinvent and change the way we do things. Business has changed and people in business need to change too. In the United States they call this 'pivoting'. It's an exciting time for the brand and customers. Technology has not only enabled us to communicate and spread knowledge about the skin more easily—both to customers and to the students who learn with us, predominantly online—it has also enabled us to get more targeted and personalise what we give each customer, hopefully enriching their experience with the brand. We are able to treat the skin with different active ingredients, machinery and techniques that might have existed 10 years ago, but have become a lot more refined, results-driven and good for the skin since then. The opportunities are endless, but equally important is the human touch we bring to our clients. This will never be replaced by technology, DIY YouTube clips or Instagram. Making the skin feel good is about high tech and the digital world, but it is equally about high touch. There are so many people burning for a greater sense of community, deeper relationships, more specialised expertise and quality ingredients. Quality, value and the experience we create speak for themselves but we live in a world of extremes and we are well placed to offer these to people, whether it's instore or online. It's up to personal choice.

Today, with globalisation, running a business means competing in a global marketplace. Once upon a time what was happening in the UK didn't matter when you were running an Australian business. Today it does. For businesses to be successful today, they need good data, speed and the ability to build new ways of doing things. Sometimes you need to

You need to follow your intuition, and with the support of data — it won't fail you.

break things to rebuild them. It requires a lot of letting go, being able to back yourself and steering the change, especially when it's what everyone has known for decades. You need to follow your intuition, and with the support of data—it won't fail you. The biggest mistakes I have made are when I haven't followed my intuition or taken too long to act on something. It just festers and the issue gets bigger.

There's a theory that you are the sum total of the five people you spend the most time with. So if you change the people you spend time with, you can hugely influence your thinking. I had the opportunity to go and do an executive course at one of the best universities in the United States, and, being surrounded by leaders who run global businesses, even after a week my mindset shifted completely from Australia to the globe—my whole mindset expanded to much bigger horizons and it enabled me to see bigger opportunities. So if you want to play at a higher level in your personal or professional life choose people to spend time with who will change your perspective.

Building resilience

How do you get yourself back up off the floor when you're down? No-one has a perfect career, or a perfect life. Building resilience, I believe, is one of the most important qualities and capacities to have in this world if you want to survive. It's about toughness and the ability to keep going. I have had to build resilience, but I never set out to do it. I hated many of the experiences that taught me to be resilient, but in hindsight they were the best gifts. I have had to be tough, otherwise I would have fallen over a long time ago. I believe it's the best thing you can teach your children and I know there is a lot of focus on resilience today.

We are all going to experience hard times and getting back up is the most important thing to do. I am fortunate that I have always had a good mindset though I certainly don't always wake up in the morning thinking 'I've got this; I'm going to nail this'. There are so many times when I have thought 'okay, I am actually in over my head and don't know how to get through this'. But I also have the belief that I will get through it eventually. My glass is always half full and I believe that there are plenty of opportunities around the corner while reminding myself that the painful, dark and hard moments do pass.

You just have to hang in there as energy and life do shift for the better. It's not always easy to prevent stressful or challenging situations but life does strengthen your ability to cope and deal with the challenges along the way. It's one of the key capabilities that I want my children to have—in fact, they have no choice! I am not an advocate for kids being wrapped up in cotton wool and protected from losing or from knowing about the tough things that can happen. This used to be called 'helicopter parenting'—now it's called 'drone parenting'. They need to be exposed (to a point) to things and experiences that will help them build a capacity to deal with the big challenges when they do come in life, while simultaneously creating a safe environment where they feel unconditional love.

While I am certainly no expert, and my kids teach me new things every day, I do believe they need the space and ability to push boundaries and take risks, with nature being the best environment to do this in; otherwise they will take risks in much more harmful places than nature. I watch my three-year-old, Darcy, jump off rocks, stand at the surf's edge, climb trees and fall over time and time again. I hope taking risks in nature will mean he doesn't need to take as many risks in the car when he learns to drive or in other destructive ways when he is older. I also try to have a sense of humour with things that happen in their life. My kids are so different. One is like a lamb: sensitive, creative, intuitive and a deep thinker. The other is more of a lion: blind courage, a risk taker, confident. They need different things and one isn't better than the other. Just different.

Being a CEO you become the one who hoses down the stressful situations and pulls people together, out of a disaster frame of mind and into a positive, action-focused mindset (such as when the GFC hit on the day I became CEO). As my dad says, 'when the going gets tough, the tough get going' (or maybe that's a song, but it's a good one). You need to believe you have the ability to get through things and a positive attitude that things will be okay, even during those unexpected crises that you just don't see coming. I make mistakes all the time. I need to recover quickly. I don't have the time to sit around and worry about what's failed—what hasn't worked. To recover, sometimes I just need to put one foot in front of the other and keep going! I can always find an opportunity in every situation. I am conscious that I am very fortunate I was born a positive person. My friends remind me that this is not the case for many people: there are so many people suffering from anxiety and depression. I realise it's not always easier said than done, so I can only speak for myself. I always try and look for opportunities and to be on the bright side. During the tough times, I think about what Ella and my grandparents went through and how much resilience was required to leave their families and move to a new country with nothing and no-one.

I believe there are two emotions: fear and love. It's fear that wakes you up at 3 am. What is the phone call you are most worried about receiving? Sometimes it's the things you worry most about that turn out fine and it's the things that were totally unexpected and you haven't spent an effort fearing that really blindside you.

Do you face it, sit in it, shine a light on it and move through it? I have learned that you need to sit in and do the things that you don't want to do first. Otherwise you get stuck in the energy of it, and you simply can't move forward. Some things can be solved in a conversation; some things take years to work through. When you face the dark stuff, the tough stuff, you come out the other side, but if you resist, what you resist persists. We all know someone who has become stuck and not able to work through a situation or a tough time in their life and they are left being defined by it. I find it helps to talk to someone about situations—usually you'll feel worse afterwards if you hold it inside than if you talk it out.

Nurturing your senses

Despite so many amazing advancements in technology and the speed at which we live our lives today, the human touch versus high tech, rituals, ceremonies and community are as important in today's world as they ever have been.

The Japanese are so great at thinking through the five senses of touch, smell, sound, taste and sight. The experience we offer a customer when they visit an Ella Baché salon has to be filled with ritual and ceremony. It goes without saying that their skin will be much healthier afterwards, they will learn something about their skin that they didn't know before, and they will also experience a beautiful hour of ritual as it's also about the connection between the therapist and the client and the experience they have. The beautiful trait that most skin therapists have in common is that they want to help people.

Layne Beachley shared a powerful story about her weekly ritual of visiting her beauty therapist when she was going through one of the darkest moments in her life. Layne's therapist was one of the only two people in her life at the time she confided in and spoke to on a deeply personal level and in some ways this saved her at that point in her life. (Her story is after chapter 2, if you haven't already read it.)

I remember receiving a letter from a lovely older lady who had been given a gift voucher from a friend for Christmas. This lady had grown up on a farm and had never had a facial before. She wrote to me sharing her happiness and the impact this experience had on her. She had not been touched or hugged for decades because she had lived on her own for so long. Having young children I sometimes crave for some personal space, but this story touched me and I always remind our therapists to never underestimate the positive impact they have on people's lives, the connection and rituals they provide and the power they have to make someone's day, above and beyond great skin.

Grounding yourself

When everything around you falls apart, you need to have a place where you can go and reboot. I have always needed the ocean to recharge myself. The moment I see it when driving home from the office is the moment I switch off. That feeling of jumping into the ocean, when everything washes off you, centres me again. I am fortunate enough that I can walk to the beach, so on warmer nights I spend an hour down there, re-centring myself, kids in tow, no phones and completely disconnected. Yoga works to re-anchor the body too and it's something I have practised since I was a teenager. I love the gentleness and flow it gives you, both mentally and physically. If I have had a tough day, I will go to a class on my way home and I'm almost guaranteed to walk out a new person!

Kids have taught me the importance of rituals and routine. They need them to feel safe and also to be able to go out and explore and take on the world. Although I work, I try hard to have a routine with them: to get home at a certain time, read them a book and do the same things every night when I can. They need certainty and predictability. The first thing Lachie asks me every morning is 'What are you doing today?' He needs to know, to predict and to feel safe.

Having kids has challenged one of my biggest anchors and that's my sleep. Busy days have always meant that I use up a lot of energy, but I got by because I was always a great sleeper. I can sleep anywhere. When I first met my now husband and we had been going out a lot, I feel asleep in the shower standing up! Lachie was a shocking sleeper; he didn't sleep through the night until he was about two years old. It totally turned me upside down because all of a sudden I had lost the ability to recharge and go again. I had never dealt with sleep deprivation before so I had been able to take on anything because I was focused, positive and had clarity. Becoming a mum quickly changed that! My first few years as a mum were the hardest. I felt like I was permanently jet lagged. With this came numerous cups of coffee each day even before 8 am — exercise dropped and carbs increased. Looking back I don't know how I survived some days at work. I learned to write a lot more down, even before having conversations, so I could structure my thoughts and retain things; otherwise I would have lost a few years of my life to sleep deprivation.

When my second son came along, everyone told us, 'don't worry you won't have another bad sleeper. You will be fine this time'. That wasn't the case. Darcy was just as bad. Our nights were spent up and down every few hours and our days started at 4 am. We even had a sleep consultant who spent three nights at our house and couldn't get Darcy to sleep through the night. Thankfully at three years old Darcy had his tonsils out and our sleep patterns changed overnight! But I approached sleep deprivation differently with Darcy. Every time I was so exhausted I could hardly walk I would jump on the treadmill at the local gym for 20 minutes and it would energise me. I kept up my yoga and didn't make myself feel guilty for taking time away from work or the kids to recharge myself—you live and you learn, right? I made sure I didn't reach for the carbs and sugar and filled myself with the good, natural, raw food that I would normally eat. Living with sleep deprivation wasn't any easier, but I learned to manage everything around it a little better. I think I would have gone on to have more kids if they had been better sleepers, but five years of sleep deprivation was enough for me and certainly for my husband.

Getting out on the trampoline or playing a game of soccer with my kids in the back yard brings me back down to earth and anchors me; there is nothing like being beaten at soccer by your five-year-old to anchor your thoughts and get back to the moment.

Rituals, routines and anchors

Rituals, routine and anchors enrich our lives. They make for a better day, a better week. I try to start my week on a Sunday night with a yoga class; it helps me re-set mentally and physically for the week ahead. If I don't have time to do this, it really affects how I feel on Monday morning. When life gets overwhelming I compartmentalise my thoughts and only focus on what I can control and what I need to deal with in that moment. There are times when you absolutely have to put your game face on and delay the thoughts that you really should be dealing with. Writing also helps me a lot. When things get overwhelming, I find getting my thoughts down on paper and expressing how I feel enables me to clear my mind and put things into perspective. I'm also a list maker. I don't always look back at my lists, but once I have a list on paper, it structures and compartmentalises my thinking. When life's busy and there is a lot going on, those lists can be broken down hourly to get moving and get stuff done. I have learned that if something needs to be dealt with or there is a problem to solve, you should deal with it as quickly as possible because it never goes away by itself.

I also try to eat healthy food and live by the 80/20 rule. If I tried 100 per cent of the time, I would set myself up to fail! I haven't eaten meat since I was 16 years old. It's a personal thing and I don't mind others eating it—I cook it for my sons and husband. But I grew up surrounded by animals: we always had dogs, I rode a horse from an early age and I fell in love with animals. I was in the Girl Guides for a year, and one of the excursions was to an abattoir—that was the end of eating meat for me. But whether you eat meat or not, healthy eating 80 per cent of the time really helps to give you the energy to live a bold and big life. Being hydrated is also important—it has a big impact on your skin. The skin, being your largest organ, is made up of mostly water, like our bodies, so we should try to drink as much water as possible. At Ella Baché we try to educate people to take care of themselves inside and out.

Some people may find routines are too repetitive, but I consider them simple daily acts that create positive habits. They are easy to put into practice and remain one thing that I can control within my day. Creating routines and anchors in your life compels you to get started, whether that's getting up and making a coffee at the same time each morning, a workout or a simple two minutes of meditation. This is the time you are able to free your mind and let it be in the present moment.

I was raised in a family where a skincare routine was drummed into me from a young age; it's now something I live and breathe and will hopefully pass on to my children. I like to think of it as a 'skin health' ritual. No matter what happens in my day, I will not miss my skin routine. I hear people say it's time consuming but my response is simple: 'your skin is your largest organ and your protective barrier—you need to look after it properly'. Especially as mums we often put ourselves last. I remember going on a trip to Japan with a girlfriend several years ago around the time they just introduced the millilitre restriction for liquids on planes. I was made to empty my hand luggage at customs and hand over my professional-sized cleanser, moisturiser and eye creams. I don't think they had ever seen anything like it!

Something as simple as creating a skin health routine or having your morning coffee at the same time each day will anchor you. What are your daily anchors? Do they bring you back to the moment?

Last year, I lost my biggest life anchor, my mum. Sadly, she became sick nine months before she passed away. I still find it very hard to write about it now—I think it takes a long time to process grief. I still remember getting the call from my brother that Mum had been taken to hospital and the specialist wanted to see us right away. I knew it wasn't good, and driving to the hospital I knew our life was about to change forever. There are no rules for when this happens and nothing can prepare you for it. But I knew Mum would be scared and I had to stay positive, calm and full of hope. The doctors wasted no time and Mum started treatment right away. I knew that Mum was very sick and had no choice but to follow the doctor's treatment plans, but I also knew enough about nutrition and alternative therapies to know you need to put as much goodness into you as well when your body is being pumped with so many intense drugs. Mum really pushed back on this, and as hard as it was I had to learn that my role now was to support her decisions and not fight against them for the first time in my life. Mum went through six months of intensive treatment and it was so painful to sit back and not be able to solve the problem. My nature is to move forward, solve problems. I am a doer. I take action, but in this situation I couldn't. Of course I could run around the edges of it, pick things up and clean things, but I wasn't going to solve this, so I had to leave it to others. I realise looking back I survived on adrenalin, often waking up and realising that it wasn't a bad dream we were in; it was my new reality and there was no escaping it. My brother and I were with Mum every day for eight months and we were there when she passed away late last year.

My biggest anchor was no longer there and it turned my life upside down. Now I belong to a new 'club' of women and men who have lost their mums. A club that I wasn't ready for, a club that is not a voluntary one. I have connected with so many amazing people during this time and sharing our stories and being open has made the journey easier. My mum was a rock and an anchor in our lives. I believe I have lived an adventurous life: not sweating the small things; not worrying too much because she did all the worrying for us and was always there, always predictable, always reliable and always thinking about her family, so it allowed me to be brave and live outside my comfort zone because she created such as safe and reliable comfort zone. Mum would call each night at 7 pm on the dot, even if I had seen her an hour before. The phone doesn't ring at 7 pm any more and I have had to learn to process the grief. I have had to learn about this new emotion that hits you out of nowhere. I have had to learn to lean on new anchors, to step out into nature when my feet need to be on the ground. Kids certainly give you the anchors you need and especially when you have to reinvent your anchors at one of the hardest times in life, but it did teach me how much you can get through. It taught me how precious life is and that you have to live life every day because you really don't know how long you have on this planet.

Life can throw you curve balls and it can also throw you amazing opportunities. Once you determine what you want to achieve, you need to surround yourself with like-minded people who have your back and are up for the ride, which I talk about in the next chapter. There will be times for celebration, there will be times when you need to dig deep and discover the resilience you never knew you had. But at the end of the day they are all experiences that teach you so much. Don't forget to challenge yourself along the way, take the time to reflect and make sure you are playing at the highest possible level.

BE BOLD
AND STEP INTO YOUR POWER

See whether any of these tips help you to determine your anchors and rituals so that you can step into your power.

* Compartmentalise your thoughts. Break things down into their simplest form.

* Fight for what matters to you.

* Be okay with setbacks and failures. Learn from your mistakes and move on.

* Get over self-doubt by talking about your wins.

* Tell young people that anything is possible — because they will grow up believing it.

* Don't drag yourself down by comparing yourself to others or getting caught up in their negativity.

* How big are your dreams? Follow your dreams, not your fears.

* Get clear on your purpose, goals and priorities, then work backwards to achieve them.

* Surround yourself with people who can lift you up and help you play at a higher level.

* Follow your intuition — it's usually right.

* Connect with your five senses regularly — it doesn't take much but it will make you feel nurtured.

(continued)

* As a working mum, the rules change every 24 hours. Keep adjusting.

* Write it down—getting things out of your head and down onto paper helps to organise your life, giving you more power and control over it.

* Use rituals and routines to help get you going each day, give your day structure and create positive habits.

* Walking and yoga ground me. What are your anchors? Discover them and live by them because they will enrich your life.

TALKING BOLD AND STEPPING INTO YOUR POWER
WITH JESSICA WATSON

F or Jessica Watson, her definition of living a bold life was not just a dream. It became a reality at a young age. Jess believes living a bold life is about challenging the status quo, not just doing the traditional things and not living what's considered a 'normal life'. I couldn't think of anyone better than Jess to interview to discover how you can push through your self-doubt and really step into your dreams and make them a reality when all the odds are against you. Thank heavens there are young trailblazers like Jess who are open to sharing their story. Here's what she had to say.

★ ★ ★

It does need to be all-consuming as you can't do things by halves. There are both positives and negatives to living a bold life. It can be very hard on the people around you but if it's your passion you have to give it your all.

It's hard to put these labels on yourself, and think of yourself as a 'bold person', but it's probably fair to say I am. Being bold is not about blowing your own trumpet. Bold is certainly a good thing but it's not always perceived to be a great thing as well, especially in Australia.

There are a lot of other little things that have felt quite scary and daunting at the time, even when you feel bold. I certainly can't go past the sailing-around-the-world-at-16 thing. And at the finish where I boldly pushed back on the prime minister as well, especially on such a public stage and platform.

The ability to make bold choices starts from an early age, and if you have been told from when you are young that you can do anything and you listen to those people who are telling you, you grow up believing that this is how things are done. You start to develop that attitude without realising and start to challenge the way things are done. You need that attitude where you're challenging norms; otherwise it's hard to be bold. Spending time talking to friends and family, half joking, half not joking, but you start to work backwards to make things possible. It is not easy and often sounds highly unrealistic, but with the right amount of sacrifice and dreams your passion becomes so great you can achieve anything.

Anything is possible, and the question becomes *Are you willing to do what it takes?*

I really do like that feeling of being stretched, looking out for opportunities and situations that give me that feeling, a feeling slightly daunting and quite simply being bold. It's not always easy; there are days and weeks where things feel overwhelming but that isn't a bad thing; it can be motivating if you learn to manage it. For example, something I learned while I was at sea, and this is something I learned from all those other adventurers and sailors, and a sports psychologist, was to focus on the next little goal on the bad days. So, when you're having a grim day, and that might be just because you didn't get a great night's sleep, it's very easy to feel overwhelmed by everything you've signed yourself up for. But, if you just say to yourself, 'no, I'm just focusing on getting through the next few hours', things become a bit more manageable. So that's something I definitely try and do to stop myself catastrophising on a bad day.

I love being very clear about my priorities, and kind of taking the time to stop and consider what they are, and making sure that those are the things I'm focusing on. It's very simple when you're obviously in the middle of something, like a voyage around the world, or planning for a voyage, because you are so single-minded that your priorities are very clear. And that kind of makes it easier in some ways. Being able to focus on a goal and those next few little steps, or those next few miles, or whatever it might be in front of you, especially when you're having a tough day. Being very clear about my priorities, sitting down at the start of every year and really taking time to think about what this year is about, and what matters.

It was tough when the most obvious kind of mistake I made at the start of my voyage was really public. The whole hitting a ship thing was really horrible, and you know it was very hard on everyone around me at the time; gosh it did happen for a reason. It's one of the key things that made me who I am, and, it set me up for the rest of the voyage. In that situation I had absolutely no choice but to share it publicly, be open about my mistakes, not trying to hide anything and taking an honest and open approach to it.

I had to accept everyone knowing everything about me for a while, but I am naturally a very private person, and I do like to protect some of that. I do choose to keep my private life private, and I suppose it's that simple.

I hate to say that I'm not a natural at anything, because everything's, you know, a learning process, I do think from a young age I have always been somebody who was never afraid to say what I think. And I think that came from having a very supportive family, and even my best friend, particularly, I think, had a huge impact on me when I was young. I felt so supported, that I could feel safe saying what I thought. So that kind of set me up for being able to do that. *When you have that single-minded focus and purpose, it's easy to be bold.*

I'm definitely at a stage now where in some ways I feel like my story is not holding me back, but it's definitely interesting because there is a big part of me that wants to move away from being the 16-year-old girl in the pink boat. I'm very proud of my achievements and the voyage, but there are so many amazing things that have made me who I am today, and ahead of me, and I really want to get to a point where I'm respected by a small number of people for what I'm doing now, rather than what I did 10 years ago.

Feeling confident is the best thing you can do to make bold decisions and putting your opinions forward, but you have to be comfortable in putting it out there, and never holding back what you think. Never being quiet if there's something you think you can contribute in any situation. Alongside that is the kind of planning, and priorities, as a total contrast. But, I think those things kind of balance themselves out pretty well. Ultimately you have to prioritise the things that are the most important.

Confidence came during the voyage, as it built up quite naturally, and just having that all-consuming purpose, it became very easy to not hold back in that situation. It's been interesting in other situations. I felt a lot more vulnerable when writing my novel, you know. This is something that, in a way, is quite personal. Putting that out there, for the world to criticise, that's where it took a bit of courage, and I had to draw on the experiences that I've had previously and going, alright, well I did it then, I can do it now. You know, I can be bold, and do this now. So it does give you confidence. You can build upon your previous situations and learnings.

It does take time, and it's not easy to do. You need a certain amount of mental discipline to not obsess over what's gone wrong. You've got to be able to move on to focusing on the future, take what you've learned from it, and keep moving forward.

I love the analogy of a tree with roots. You've got to put out these beautiful, big, strong roots to help you feel confident when there's a strong wind, so it doesn't knock you over. The tree roots, for me, are having that support network of people around you. But you also have to back yourself. Be audacious. I love the idea of audacity, and I think it goes very much hand-in-hand with being bold. So, why shouldn't I? You know, you should ask yourself that question. Look at all your heroes in whatever field that might be and ask yourself why shouldn't I be one of those people? And then ask yourself, what will it take? That's for everyone to work out in their own time.

But sometimes I also need to throw out all my priorities for the day and just go and have fun!

Chapter 5
OWN YOUR TRIBE

There is no possession more valuable
than a good and faithful friend.
Socrates

How can you find a tribe of like-minded people who have your back? Finding your tribe enables you to create something much bigger than you would individually. In his brilliant book *Tribes,* marketing guru Seth Godin says that 'leaders lead when they take positions, when they connect with their tribes, and when they help the tribe connect to itself'. Connect people in your social network who have common interests; give them access to the information and resources that they need; and let them know that you're available if they need help. We all know someone who is brilliant at doing this!

When you run a business the path can be a lonely one, unless you choose otherwise. It's a path where you're guaranteed to be challenged every single day; it's a path where not many lines are straight and change is the only certainty. I am a free spirit at heart and in many ways would be happy being a hippie. People give me energy and I need to work and collaborate with people. So for me it is important to build close and lasting relationships. That's how I best play to my strengths. Of course, I have learned to make the hard calls and do it quickly when things aren't working or get tough, but I also knew that the stereotypical female role models of the 1980s and 1990s in their power suits, with super-bitch personalities, were never going to be me. If I was going to lead a business I had to create my own style and my own way. That meant building close relationships and a culture that is an extension of the family.

Having a tribe of supportive, open, honest and non-judgemental women around you makes life so much easier and in many ways you can do anything if you have this support. I think it's a fallacy that women don't want to support each other. In my experience it's certainly not been the case. Maybe it's a sign of the times that women can hold on to their femininity and be strong at the same time.

> **Having a tribe of supportive, open, honest and non-judgemental women around you makes life so much easier and in many ways you can do anything if you have this support.**

Women of the 1960s and 1970s fought so hard for equality and in so many ways we have come so far but in other ways we still have a long way to go. In the 1980s and 1990s women really did have to become like men if they wanted a successful career. They even had to look and act more like men: suits, haircuts and the way they spoke. We can now celebrate the fact that we no longer have to do this and can be ourselves. We can also be kind to other women, have them in our tribe and not work against them. At the same time when I am in a room full of men, I don't want to be that woman who puts barriers up on them and changes the way they behave, unless their behavior is inappropriate. I just want equality and for people to have an equal contribution, regardless of sex. Real relationships and a strong tribe can only ever be built if you can be yourself, and connect on a real and deeper level. Putting your energy into defending, politicking and building a wall around yourself will never result in healthy relationships on a professional or personal level. There has to be trust, and there have to be shared values and beliefs. I believe we all have a strong instinct and desire to belong to our 'tribe' of like-mind people.

I was fortunate to hear Elizabeth Broderick, who was the Australian Sex Discrimination Commissioner for over eight years. Elizabeth believed it's not the women who need to become more like men to survive in the business world; it's the culture, systems and structures—or space, as I like to call it—that need to change to accommodate women. Unfortunately this is still not the case for many organisations, which still set up in very masculine ways. We know that a lot of successful women are still opting out of the workforce and the kids or elderly parents are often cited as the reason. The main reason is they simply are not valued. Many organisations are now working to quotas and targets to increase the number of women on boards or C-suites. This is not going to solve the issue. The issue is around establishing an inclusive culture and one of valuing individuals and diversity. In my experience many working mums will get the job done, and get the job done amazingly—but give them a job and a deadline and don't except them to bundy on at 9 am and off at 5 pm. I am fortunate that I work in an inclusive culture and while I work just as hard as anyone (and the rest!) it's in my DNA. I do it because I do it in my way. I don't think I could do what I do if I had to conform to traditional big-corporate structures and norms. The future of work needs to be more projects-based, and more outcomes-based. It's come a long way in the past 10 years but it has a long way to go. I remember starting my career in advertising. We worked hard, the hours were long and you wouldn't even consider working from anywhere but the office. People still smoked at their desks; there was a 'trolley lady' who brought around food and a café so you didn't have to leave the office for breakfast, lunch or dinner. Don't get me wrong: I loved it as we worked hard and played hard, but the idea of working from somewhere else just didn't exist even in the mid 1990s. Thankfully, many workplace spaces are evolving to allow for more like-minded women to belong—to give their all to work and to be mums too. We no longer have to pretend we belong to a workplace, culture or tribe that doesn't enable us to be who we need to be. Over the years I have met many incredible women who I would consider to be part of this 'tribe' of working mums who can talk about their business strategy and challenges, and also their kids' day, all in the same conversation and in the same work space. This wouldn't ever have happened, as Elizabeth Broderick so rightly pointed out, if women had adapted to be more like men and the work space of the past.

Choosing your tribe

Sadly, still to this day there are not many female CEOs, or female CEOs who are mums too. Luckily for me, I knew one of the first things I needed to find when I took this path was a few people

I could trust and reach out to when the shit hit the fan—people who were part of my 'tribe' and really understood. In Oprah Winfrey's words, 'surround yourself with only people who are going to lift you higher'. Luckily I have my dad, who I talk to nearly every day. Sometimes I know he doesn't feel like listening as his passion is painting, but he still listens. Sometimes that's all that needs to happen. But other times, I need others who aren't family. I report to a board and while it's not unconditional, they are there for support or to give me direction.

My first and only mentor is a wonderful woman (who a friend introduced me to). She is a mum and entrepreneur who truly knows what it's like to walk a mile in my shoes. I spent three years with her, meeting once a week, and if it was up to me I probably still would be meeting her once a week. She basically fired me, telling me it was time to move on and find someone else. At the time I thought, 'Are you serious? Isn't it my role to decide when it's time to move on?' The good thing is we became good friends so I haven't lost her in my life.

I'm also fortunate that I love what I do. Of course, there are hard days and things that I would rather not do, but because I am passionate about work, and it's part of who I am, it's become a lifestyle. I don't turn on at 9 am and turn off at 5 pm. I am always working and it's not a bad thing. I am always thinking about things—new ideas, how we can do things differently—and looking at the broader world for inspiration. I think people associate work with stress and it being a chore. It's not like that for me—it's a lifestyle. Life and work are one and the same for me. I have chosen that work is part of my life and I don't turn it on and off.

The wonderful part about belonging to a big network like Ella Baché is that you get to meet and collaborate with some incredible people—and 70 per cent of those people are women. They're inspiring, especially the younger therapists who are about to embark on owning and running a salon for the first time. But equally, the older women, who remain open to changes, technology and new innovations. Their cup is always half full! Their passion for their craft and openness to learn is awesome. There are thousands of people who put their heart and soul into the Ella Baché brand: therapists, salon owners, suppliers and many others. This means there is always someone to turn to if you have a question or need help—someone to share ideas and aspirations with during challenges and times of learning.

Ella Baché has created life friendships and many are like sisters. It has allowed people to connect with each other where they would not otherwise have made connections. The more you put into it, the more you get out of it. You can't force these networks and relationships; you can't go in there wanting to get something back instantly. Relationships have to form naturally over time. Trust and respect can't be forced. You have to work on it and sometimes there is an instant connection, while sometimes a connection only comes over a period of years.

So often we think it's our skills we need to develop, or further education we need to embark on, but often it's more important to surround yourself with the right people. How often do you find yourself spending 80 per cent of your time on poor performers or negative people? Over the years I have learned that I first always see the good and potential in everyone, but not everyone has the same wants, desires or values—and that's okay, but it's important to recognise that quickly and move on. Don't try to rescue them. Don't try and force the relationship to work. They may not want it. Surround yourself with people who can support you to achieve your goals or vision, or people who will be kind, honest and give you that support unconditionally and expand you by bringing different but equal strengths to the table. At the end of the day, choose your tribe wisely as the people who you surround yourself with will have an enormous impact on your happiness and success.

Over the years I have found these people both by chance and organically. But there have also been times when I have clearly identified a gap I had to fill and gone out there and found a mentor or role model or network that has given me the support I needed to achieve my goals. Either way the people I am closest to in my life have all been a big part of who and where I am in my life today.

Pay it forward

At Ella Baché we put a lot of focus on holding events that encourage deep relationships, networking and time spent together to build our tribe. A lot of time is put aside for yearly conferences, award nights and events, the purpose being to create relationships but also to learn. Show up: what you put in you will get out. Be positive, be genuine, ask questions and be friendly. You never know what someone is going through in their personal world. Everyone's life is complex, and there are many times when I haven't slept (thanks, kids!) but I wouldn't ever tell anyone how tired I was or how I just wanted to be at home in bed instead of being there. I would always show up and remain positive.

My favourite annual event is the 'Ella Awards'. It's always a huge night with a few hundred people gathered to recognise those Ella Baché business owners and therapists who have achieved so much throughout the previous year. It's a night full of passion, laughter, tears and lots of great, close relationships. So many are so passionate about Ella Baché and they put their heart and soul into what they do, and achieve great things. For me, it's truly a privilege that my heritage and family has been able to create an environment for opportunity.

I have had the privilege of being part of so many girls' journeys as they go from their early twenties as young passionate beauty therapists, and their ambitions and confidence grow to wanting to run their own business. They learn and grow **Show up: what you put** as they open their own Ella Baché business **in you will get out.** and take on running a business in their own right: managing a team, clients, marketing, financials, training, leases and suppliers. To watch them go from young girls to businesswomen is awesome. They often go on to get married and have kids and I often feel like the mother hen. I certainly don't claim to know it all, but being able to share the experience with incredible Ella Baché women (and men) is such a great part of the company.

The 'old is gold' tribe

I am fortunate to have found my tribe of girlfriends when I was 12. We went to high school together and still talk nearly every day. We are all very different, and among us there are singers, directors, photographers, mums, teachers, corporate high fliers and architects. But all that goes out the window when we come together because we care deeply for each other. There has never been any competition or bitchiness among us—and never any judgement. We laugh hard together and it never matters how much time has passed, it's always 'straight in'. We are all so different, but our values are the same and that's the glue that holds us together. Half of the girls have moved out of Sydney to escape the intensity of life, but we come together at least once a year for a weekend away. No kids, no partners. It's *so* good for the soul: we eat, laugh, drink, walk and talk. We always end up in sessions where we just talk and open up to each other like we would open up to no-one else. It's Chatham House rules and we need this time and space to show vulnerabilities, imperfections and laugh at each other's stories and experiences. It makes it real. Too often you think the world needs to see perfection, but that's not where the depth sits.

Seek mutual support

The world is moving at such an incredible speed now, and solving problems needs to happen on the spot with innovative and creative thinking. I need to learn and collaborate with my team or tribe at work. But it also applies to my friends. How many nights do you find yourself sitting around solving the world's problems together? The power of many minds is so much greater than just my own. I have always had a curious mind. I used to drive my mum nuts from a young age by always asking 'why'. Mum would often answer 'because I said so'. Of course that wasn't the response I needed, so I kept pushing and pushing. This later transferred to my teachers and I wouldn't always buy into the answer they provided either, putting me in hot water. I have taken this attribute and now use it to push my tribe at work. I know this drives some of them mad as I push against the status quo and just because we did it last year is never a reason why we should do it this year. Maybe I need to learn to let go and that some things are okay being left unturned. Past success used to be the best predictor of future success, but for the first time in history this is no longer the case. We live in a world with unprecedented futures. So how do you navigate this as a mum, a CEO? By surrounding myself with people who support me, and can problem solve with me to solve some of the issues that keep me awake at night. You can't do it alone.

Business models have to change every five years if they are to stay relevant, so as a business leader, I therefore need to be the catalyst of this change and also change every five years. That's a 20 per cent change needed each year to stay relevant as a leader. The only way to fuel this change is through new learnings and knowledge. You can't stand still; if you stand still you are going backwards. I spend a lot of time committed to learning.

Money has never motivated me, creation and creativity have always motivated me, but at the same time I can't do things for free, or not put a value on myself or my skills. This is so common to so many women I have met who have amazing skills and lifelong experiences with value to bring to different situations, but they undervalue themselves time and time again. Putting a value on your skills is one thing, but putting a value on your time is another thing. I spend a lot of time reading blogs and articles and listening to podcasts. The fantastic thing about social media and the digital platforms is that it's delivered to you in personalised bite-size chunks, rather than trying to read that book that's been sitting on the bedside table for six months. The trade-off, though, is it's so personalised today that you're often not exposed to different viewpoints. We usually belong to social communities with only people and content that is in line with yours, which can lead to uniformity, shallow thinking and less meaning. Social media rather than mass media is very targeted in nature and therefore you turn off anything that challenges or doesn't appeal to you. This is why I challenge it. You should keep seeking out information that challenges you and is thought provoking—it may be books, movies or travel to different cultures—to keep an open mind and ensure things challenge your views and knowledge. The same need for diversity goes with the group of people or the tribe of people surrounding you. The greater the diversity, the deeper the thinking and the more chance of coming up with innovative ways of doing things.

I was exposed to personal development courses and information—from Tony Robbins to Robert Kiyosaki—from a young age growing up with a dad who encouraged this continuously. I remember attending a 'money for you' seminar when I was about 17. An SBS crew had filmed it and turned it into a documentary on cults. My mum just happened to watch this show and I was banned from going to any more of these courses...as they say, horses for courses!

The world changes so quickly and in today's society you have to keep learning and growing—it's now considered one of the greatest indicators of success. I was fortunate to stumble across a great global organisation (Young Presidents' Association) that provides lifelong learning for young CEOs. It was one of those meant-to-be coincidences that took place when I was talking to our graduates at an end-of-year ceremony. A man in the audience approached me at the end of the evening and invited me for a coffee to learn about this organisation. I never looked back. There are over 100 members in Sydney—sadly only eight women—and we are exposed to unique learning experiences and are part of a forum group that meets monthly to discuss business, personal or family issues, all of which holds you to account and provides support.

The dream team

My team have their own learning objectives within their annual goals, so we all keep growing and learning and can see the complex issues of the world on a broader level and from different perspectives. It's not only about the knowledge you acquire: it's equally important how you do something. And it's not just what you do and how you do it, but also how you make someone *feel*. Learning that your impact on others may not always match your intention means you have to be aware and mindful. I love the saying by American poet Maya Angelou, 'I've learned that people will forget what you said, people will forget what you did, but people will never forget how you made them feel'.

It's not just what you do and how you do it, but also how you make someone *feel*.

I believe it's human nature to want to belong: to be part of a team or a tribe, a close group of people who accept one another and support each other and have each other's back. The term 'tribe' can sound prehistoric, but it's the same as having a sense of community and family. No-one likes to feel like they don't belong or are the outcast or black sheep in the group. They want to belong, to feel loved and supported. Belonging to a great group of people definitely gives you a greater sense of meaning, and encourages you to pursue your vision and a better life as a result.

So choose your tribe wisely. They have an enormous impact on who you become as a person, and you certainly wouldn't want to choose to hang out with negative, nasty people and become one. It takes both recognising the amazing people who walk into your life naturally and going out and seeking people who can help support you to achieve your dreams.

BE BOLD
AND OWN YOUR TRIBE

How can you find like-minded people who have your back? Here are some tips.

* Choose your tribe wisely. The people you choose will have an enormous impact on your happiness.
* Collaborate with people, be honest and upfront and work through solutions together.
* Focus on things that are important to people in your tribe. People always give hints.
* Social media can be a great way to kept connected to people in today's busy world, but make sure it's not the only way, as it doesn't build depth and meaning.
* If you say you're going to do something, then the best thing you can do is to commit to it (sometimes it's the kindest thing you can do too).
* Look for people who will expand you and help you grow.
* Trust your gut feeling about someone. Sometimes you meet someone new and you feel like they are an old friend.

TALKING BOLD AND OWNING YOUR TRIBE
WITH KYM ELLERY

had the pleasure of collaborating with fashion designer Kym Ellery a number of years ago when we launched the new Ella Baché collection worn by thousands of Australian therapists. Kym designed, styled and priced the collection still worn today.

Kym, now based in Paris, started her business in 2007 and 10 years on became the second Australian designer to be granted entry into Paris Fashion Week's official program. What is so apparent with Kym is her passion for both the creativity and the loyalty of the people around her, who are instrumental to the brand's success. The intimacy and very personal nature of this has meant it was critical to find the right people, with the right values to work with and support her.

★ ★ ★

Launching Ellery and having the ambition and passion to really do it, often meant following my gut instinct and doing things differently from other people or the social norm. In the beginning, what I needed to do was quite bold, looking back, but at the time it was more about achieving my dream and knowing that you only have one life and you've got to make it the best life that you can. It took confidence and I've been very lucky to have a lot of loyal people around me, but also having the emotional intelligence whether it is in your work, in business or in your personal life. You need to be able to have a good eye for people who share the right values and who will be committed to the project. Values are really important. People who have these are honest, hardworking and positive. They're all things that I think I value the most and I want those same qualities in my team and the people around me. So, I'm always searching for people who have these qualities naturally.

It's a very big responsibility to own a business, as you know, and I have had moments over the years where I've felt extremely overwhelmed. In those moments, it's important to have the right people around you: your team, your family and your friends. Just to be able to talk and ground you, work through difficult periods, or find a solution and create strategies together. I think that's one of the most important things through all of it. It's all about celebrating the wins together, and making sure that there's a sense of accomplishment. The sense of accomplishment that comes after a project is really enjoyable. I think fashion is such a roller coaster. It involves a lot of hard work and there are intense periods throughout the year, panicking and worrying at the beginning when you're about to launch a collection, but then in the end it always goes ahead—always goes well. And everyone's there to celebrate at the end together.

I like to talk through problems and find solutions together. For me there's always a solution. So, I'm not afraid to sometimes just be defeated in an issue we are discussing. I think it also takes a mature and evolved person to be able to handle this process, which is what I'm always trying to be.

I really rely on my right-hand team members in the business to find those solutions together and work together. I mean, teamwork sounds cheesy, but it's just so important. And being a good leader as well—being positive and remaining in the right frame of mind to be able to overcome the challenges and have that strength for you and everyone around you.

I think people have it instinctively and that other qualities come from experience. People have different strengths and this is why it's important to choose the right people to complement one another. Developing your own style and ability to be confident and bold in a positive way really depends on how you express that boldness. I think it's important to always be elegant and respectful. We are coming out of a time where women are really starting to speak up for equality, but there's still a huge pay gap issue. There's still sexism in a lot of industries. And I think women had overcompensated in the past—they almost had to. But I think we're in a time now where they don't need to. They're becoming more and more aware that there should be equality and that they can ask about equality without coming across in a pushy or negative way.

What stops people now from backing themselves and following their passion is society and a lack of confidence. And I think that's one thing about being an Australian: we're lucky to have a youthful nation, and we're not bogged down by a heavy history or social structures in which you have to stay in your lane. We're really encouraged, as a nation, to do what we want, and think freely and that's what I think is one of the advantages of being an Australian. And that's something that I also thank for helping me make the bold moves that I have made over the years. But on the flip side, being in Australia really held our business back, and me as well, as an individual, which is sad because I think Australia's such an amazing place—but, you know, we see over and over again that people who have a creative ambition or ambition in any field tend to leave to fulfil that ambition. Because Australia is a remote place and, in my case, is such a small market for my industry. It was a huge challenge, as well, trying to deal with the time zones.

Since I've moved to France, I've just made time for mindfulness and doing yoga, or exercising and meditating. And all those things, I think, are really important to keep you grounded and focused. Because you need to be in a healthy state of mind to be able to think clearly and tackle the many issues that life throws at you. Especially now with social media, being exposed 24/7, and as it's such an important part of a brand, you need to have a unique voice and a unique style and purpose. But being visible on social media has not always been something that was natural at first, and it's something I'm still working on. I just really do it for the brand. But over the years my personal life and business life have become very combined even in the moments where you should be sharing them, in the lead-up to a show, but you're actually drowning in work and finishing touches. And then, other moments where you actually have some time to yourself, where you can be a little bit more open and share those personal moments.

I feel much more comfortable with that now than I did, and I think that's something that develops in life as you mature and grow up as well. But the many challenges that business and life have thrown at me along the way have also really matured me and given me confidence. Some of the most challenging times have left me feeling incredibly grateful because of what they gave me, or how aware I felt afterwards (or how much less intimidated I was by certain types of people). There's always a positive side, too, I think.

When I started it, I always knew that I wanted it to be a luxury brand—one of the first from Australia, if not the first for the field—in the space in which I wanted it to exist and I wanted to show it in Paris. I also like to think that when I started and had that intention there wasn't any other way, any other path that I was going to take. I just knew that it would take time, and I knew that there would be various steps. I really know that I have now achieved everything that I said I wanted to do for the first time. That's really kind of funny as I'm actually living that life now, having accomplished those things and being in a place where I want to be.

So, don't let anyone tell you otherwise. I had people try to tell me not to do things that I ended up doing anyway. And it was those things that took me one step closer to living my dream. So, just make a plan and do it. Be sure of yourself and confident in yourself that you can achieve what you want.

Chapter 6
OWN YOUR SKIN

Ella, I loved your abandon, whether it was in your chemistry
or the chemistry of love, your concern, your giving—
I remember thinking, 'that's living'.
Edith Hallas

How do you fully own the skin you're in to live a bold life?

The skin is your largest organ; it helps you do remarkable things so you want it to be the healthiest it can be as it takes you through the story of your life. It's the story the world sees. When you look in the mirror you see a story on your face; we all do. Do you see laughter lines in your face, stretch marks on your tummy or freckles on your nose from all your summertime adventures?

Makeup has never been important to anyone in my family, including me. I think people are surprised when they meet us, as we are more comfortable with no makeup and bare feet. The brand and family values have been built not on makeup but on a deep understanding of the needs of individual skins using a scientific approach. Not vanity, but healthy skin.

I remember the first time the expectations others had on my family hit home. I was quite young and there was a *Vogue* shoot with Kristy Hinze at Palm Beach. The editor at the time was a local. He knew my dad well and wanted to borrow our Clydesdale horse, Olive, for the shoot. So we took Olive down to Palm Beach and although we had been introduced to the crew as the family behind the Ella Baché brand, they simply didn't believe it, as we were not what they were expecting. I think they thought of us as the 'horse wranglers', which was fine with us as we loved our animals!

At high school I was always in trouble for arriving at school with untidy hair. I was sent straight to the year mistress' office to sort it out every morning. She then found out what my family did and her attitude towards me immediately changed. I never understood this behaviour from people. Luckily I had the confidence to own it, and my 'f**k it' attitude always got me through.

Recently I was invited back to the school for the first time to talk to the senior students for International Women's Day. As I walked through the school gates, I immediately felt like I was in trouble again thanks to all those years of judgement—of attempts to squeeze me into the mould of the perfect family. It was never going to work. I was pleasantly surprised at how much the school had changed, leaving behind some of those conservative, judgemental ways and learning to celebrate differences and individuals and empower them for it, rather than trying to erase them. It took me until my early twenties to realise that everyone is so worried about what others think of them that they don't worry about you. That realisation was such a relief and it gave me the freedom to stop worrying about what others thought I looked like.

Love your skin

The celebration of the individual and owning the skin you're in is deeply important to me. Healthy skin gives you confidence.

The beauty industry has gone through enormous change in Australia over the past few years. It has been heavily influenced by the rise of social media, and invasive services such as Botox and fillers have grown enormously in popularity because of it. It used to be that only celebrities or older women had these treatments or cosmetic surgery, but young girls—even teens—are now heavy users of it. To erase your differences and uniqueness only brings insecurity, and losing self-esteem can cause great damage. Diversity brings so much to life.

There is so much pressure on young girls today to erase their differences and with the rise of what I call 'Fast Food Beauty', Botox, fillers and other invasive treatments have become so accessible. There are many social media influencers who get treatments for free in return for promoting the services on their Instagram account. Walk into a shopping centre anywhere in Australia and you can get fillers in your lips for $5 in five minutes.

Diversity brings so much to life.

No regulations, no rules and no boundaries. While I believe there is a place for these kinds of treatments, a society that is constantly told to erase its natural or unique beauty doesn't sit well with me. Owning the skin you're in is the most empowering thing you can do because it tells the story of who you are. Many of the young girls who heavily use these treatments don't understand the longer term impact and many still have bad skin! Having fillers or Botox doesn't override the need to protect and treat your skin; they are complementary and a little bit goes a long way. Enhance what you look like, but don't try and erase it. I believe there is definitely a role for these treatments as there is for skin products and treatments, but it needs to be administered by a qualified practitioner. Many countries around the world only allow doctors to perform invasive services and regulate the use of the drugs. The Australian medical and health department is working hard on tightening up regulations and in my opinion it can't happen fast enough to ensure people have the expertise they need when going down this path.

To erase your differences and uniqueness only brings insecurity and losing out on self-esteem can cause great damage.

We have always set the standard for the segment in the industry in which we operate. Ella Baché therapists set the standards high: they know about skin and the science of the skin; they know the products, the ingredients and the impact of the ingredients on the skin. They understand the techniques required to combine technologies such as laser, IPL and LED with skin products and treatment plans—that's why we continue to get the results we do without harming the skin. People come to us for this expertise, and we aim to teach our customers something new about their skin every time they visit us. I hope the same standards can be driven across other areas of the beauty industry to protect people in the future, especially younger girls who haven't yet embraced their own unique beauty.

Finding yourself as a CEO of a skincare company in a time when you can change just about everything about your physical appearance has encouraged me to deeply consider what our stance and point of view is. Ella Baché's position doesn't cast doubt or judgement on different approaches to treating your skin, but we simply stay focused on what we do well and that's celebrating individuality rather than uniformity to develop and innovate non-invasive products and treatments to promote healthy skin and be the 'best version of yourself', not looking like someone else.

Riding the digital disruption wave

'Disruption' is one of the most frequently used words in today's society. Technology and globalisation have disrupted the way we do things and changed our lives forever. At Ella Baché we have changed the way we shop, book appointments, communicate and educate. The thought of driving disruptive change and leading a business through the most disruptive times in history is enough to make most people turn around and go back to bed. It's not for the faint-hearted. Technology has transformed our lives, the way we communicate, the way we work, the way we run our businesses and the way we treat our skin. Like all businesses, Ella Baché and I — as the leader of the change — have to be bold and lead the business through the change so our customers and future customers continue to fall in love with the brand long into the future. With this disruption comes enormous opportunity and never before has it been easier to reach people with social media and digital platforms. You either curl up and put your head in the sand and let the world change around you, or you embrace the change and make the most of it and get energised by the possibilities of innovation. Of course the latter is the only option and has always been the Ella Baché way. For our family, money has never been the driving force of the business. It has always been creativity, growth and people. We have had to learn to not give it away and be okay with standing our ground and making sure the right value exchange occurs at every transaction. We are not like the previous generation who because of the Great Depression could not spend. I remember standing on the footpath in New York with Ella around her ninetieth birthday. I was young and naive to her past experiences. Growing up in the Great Depression had affected how she lived her life even in her later years. I went to hail a cab, and Ella shrieked 'What? Do you think you are rich or something?' and off we went to the bus stop!

Emulating Ella and Dixie

I often reference the disruptive times Ella lived through in the 1930s and 1940s, pre and during World War II. She left her family when she left Czechoslovakia — at a time when there were no mobile phones and no social media networks — knowing that the world would never be the same again.

While the 1930s in Paris was a time of enormous disruption and anxiety with the uncertainty of war, it was also a time of invention, when many of the iconic skincare and beauty companies — such as Estée Lauder and Helena Rubinstein — appeared. Though the industry was still in its infancy, these pioneering women knew each other. The difference was that while Estée Lauder and Helena Rubinstein were marketing, sales and business women first and foremost, Ella was a chemist driven by science and creation. But it was my grandma Edith ('Dixie') Hallas who dedicated her life to understanding the biology and functionality of the skin. They worked as a team: my grandma translating the needs of the skin to Ella who would then formulate products based on Dixie's brief. They never innovated for the sake of it or to make more money, and they most certainly didn't do it to follow trends. The innovation stemmed from the health of the skin, at the base level the skin's cells. Dixie put her heart and soul into knowing all about the skin, constantly studying and learning. She was also very conscious of the changed conditions, and the way the environment influenced our skin's needs, especially the harsh Australian sun. It was her lifelong commitment to learning that made her a success. Later in life I have realised how critical continuous learning is to your own success, no matter what you are doing. The mantra we live by still today at Ella Baché is the belief that 'no two skins are alike' and every skin is as unique as a thumbprint. This principle goes for people too. Everyone is different.

A metamorphosis took place in the 1930s. Ella and Dixie had fallen in love with each other's passions. The skin and its wonderful function at an epidermal layer became the platform for creation. The same problem on a different skin needs a different treatment. Different skin conditions need different solutions and products. It goes much further and deeper than just classifying skin as oily, dry or combination. A treatment and product solution also depends on your lifestyle, the food you eat or don't eat and a skin program prescribed especially for the individual. Ella had many letters from women all over the world who wrote to her about their personal skin problems, wanting to learn more. Knowing that Ella Baché

The mantra we live by still today at Ella Baché is the belief that 'no two skins are alike'.

has been able to help many women around the world continues to make us just as happy as they are; having great, healthy skin gives you confidence. So many women have tried so many products and spent an enormous amount of money—without first understanding their skin—jumping straight to a product that in many cases had worked for a friend or family member. Today, we continue to have so many women contact us, mostly by email and social media.

The world of chemistry is extremely complex and it was an immensely fascinating one to Ella. Even if we knew all the elements used in a product, it's hard to appreciate (unless you're a chemist!) the changes and interactions that result in every given product. The more I work with different chemists and formulations, the more I appreciate the genius behind what Ella created in her formulations. Ella knew when formulating a product it depended on the nature of active agents, including molecular size, structure, pH in solution, lipid/water solubility and distribution behaviour. It's then about the nature of the vehicle that transports the active ingredients through the skin and the type of emulsion and the properties of it. Anyone can formulate cosmetics and it is simple to make a cosmetic (especially today when there are millions of recipes available on the internet). But a cosmetic that is like a pharmaceutical is something quite different. In a world full of allergies where products claim to be 'hypoallergenic', there is still a chance that an allergic reaction can occur. Ella Baché has always formulated products that very rarely create these reactions due to the quality of the ingredients, and that these ingredients are as pure from the source as possible. The real results happen when therapists are committed to the knowledge of how the ingredients interact with the skin cells.

Throughout her life, Ella stood behind her approach to skin health and formulations even though when trends came and went, pressure to conform did too. It was Ella's tenacity and belief in her products that earned Ella Baché's products trust and respect and allowed them to stand the test of time.

I love the stories of some of Ella's early inventions. Many people don't know that she invented some of the most widely used and recognised ingredients in the cosmetic and skincare industry today. Ella discovered hyaluronic acid and alpha-hydroxyl acid (AHA)—which is an ingredient of Ella Baché's iconic Crème Tomato—with a scientist in New York many decades ago. The professor in charge of the laboratory had known Ella for many years; he approached her to conduct research using this molecule on the skin. The molecule's specific capacity is to adhere to, surround and protect the moisture content in tissue cells. For seven years Ella researched it and subsequently used it in her skincare formulations. Ella invented fruit acids after observing peasant girls' skin and beauty routines. They used sliced tomatoes to clear blotchy skin. It turned out that lyophilised tomatoes were a wonderful ingredient for treating sensitive and oily skins.

> **It was Ella's tenacity and belief in her products that earned Ella Baché's products trust and respect and allowed them to stand the test of time.**

Ella wasn't driven by sales or marketing strategy and she would never sell her products to people she didn't like or she believed didn't have values aligned with hers. Because of this, Ella's name cropped up consistently among skincare cognoscenti and when they remarked on her success she would shrug it off; accolades didn't interest her.

Times have changed. Ingredients have changed. While some have stood the test of time, others just wouldn't be appealing today. One product, which is no longer around (you will know why in a minute), was called Mask Sanguin. For centuries, women have used all kinds of things for their skin and looks. As far back as the Roman times women were using slices of raw meat (definitely not appealing to a vegetarian!) as beauty packs. A leading chemist in the 1930s wanted to bring this idea to a product, and to create a product using the blood of beef. Ella Baché was approached to create this product and so she produced a mask based on purified haemoglobin. It became a top seller in the 1930s called Mask Sanguin ('sanguin' is French for 'blood'). Can you imagine this today?

In the world of mass production, there is still a need for the highest quality raw materials derived from nature: vitamins, herbs, essential oils, extract minerals and tissue molecules. Technological advancement has meant these emulsions and delivery systems have become like medical-grade formulas and a lot more sophisticated, but the basic principles don't change. It is not enough to just have great products…you have to know the skin first! 'Know your product, but first know your skin' is another mantra we live by today!

'Know your product, but first know your skin' is another mantra we live by today!

Today the brand is a lot bigger in size and the products and treatments are not as crude due to the technological advancements in ingredients and science; deepened knowledge of the skin; and technologies in treatment machinery. Although, in saying that, a few of Ella's original formulas are some of our bestsellers still today. One of her favourites was Crème Intex, which was totally revolutionary and transforms dry skin. Made from fish oil, which is a powerful stimulant for cell regeneration, the cream is totally absorbed into dry skin and transforms it into healthy, normal skin. I still can't live without this product in my daily routine, especially in winter. It is one of the best formulas, based on basic principles that have not changed.

Your skin tells a story: the lines, the freckles — everything about it. It reflects how you have chosen to live your live, so ask yourself, 'Who wrote your story? Your parents, your partner, your kids?' You need to own your story and be okay with the skin you're in to truly own it.

Never let them ignore you

Beauty therapist Dixie and her lawyer husband, George, moved to Australia in 1939 and she set up a cubicle in the back of a hairdressing salon in the city of Sydney. Dixie always said, 'I am me and no-one else. You are you and no-one else. Our biological makeup is as individual as our thumbprint'. In the 1940s no-one in Australia knew about skin care; it was all about makeup. Her first clients were from Europe as only women from the continent knew about beauty therapy. It was not an industry or service that had existed in Australia.

It wasn't until after World War II that Ella and Dixie truly connected again. They reconnected their passions, Ella formulating products with the highest quality ingredients and Dixie continuing her research of the cells and deepening her understanding of the skin, functionality and biology. It was the beginning of building an iconic brand and business.

In 1954, Ella developed the first cold wax strips for hair removal. They were calico strips with wax-like honey on them. Ella's husband, Ernest, being an archaeologist and art collector, had been on a trip to Egypt where he observed that women were using calico to remove hair from their legs. Ella was excited to learn about it and developed the first wax strip at a time when there was only an awful-smelling, difficult-to-use resin available to remove hair. The wax strips worked instantly! So with this product in hand, Dixie, full of fear, walked into David Jones in Elizabeth Street, Sydney, and asked where she could find the cosmetic buying office. She entered the office and met with a very tall, thin and elegant lady, Miss Philips, who looked like an empress. But she was all action and without too many words, pulled up her skirt, put one leg on the chair and said 'show me'. So Dixie quickly waxed all the hair off her legs. She was so impressed she arranged a small advertisement in *The Sydney Morning Herald* every Tuesday and Thursday where new products would be featured. She also arranged a small counter and a little beauty room for Dixie ... and the rest is history.

One by one, the Ella Baché products were introduced into David Jones alongside the other big cosmetic houses of the day, such as Helena Rubinstein. The Ella Baché promise was different as Dixie knew a lot about different individual skin conditions, the skin's problems and functions and she had a deep understanding of the right products to get results. The new wax strips were like nothing ever seen before, which gave her a good start. Ella Baché and Dixie earned the trust of the customers and sales began to grow. Today we have one of the longest standing relationships with David Jones.

Soon after, our regular customers offered to build Dixie a beauty salon because they saw how much she loved what she did. While women knew about hairdressing and makeup, skin care and treatments had a long way to go. In the meantime, the brand continued to grow in David Jones. The products were packed off in boxes from Dixie's house to the David Jones warehouse. But it reached a point where the business had outgrown the house so Dixie and George found a two-bedroom office in Artarmon. The kitchenette became the lab and the harsh Australian environment the inspiration.

Many of Dixie's Australian clients looked older than people of the same age in Europe, with skin conditions that were also different. She realised that this was due to the damage the sun had caused to their skin, in particular their hands and décolleté, and it was nothing like she had ever seen before in Europe. This became the focus of her research and motivated her to develop a zinc oxide sunscreen, which was an instant success. Dixie always said 'protection and prevention'. You had to protect your skin from the sun to prevent ageing. That was always the first step and if you could only use one product, a good sun-care product was the best form of anti-ageing. In 1972 the first sunscreen was launched.

Next was the cleanser, to ensure the right pH balance of the skin. Dixie always saw the skin as a delicate canvas and the right cleanser was the critical first step for skin health. She always believed that 'you had to know your products, but first you had to know the skin'. Aligned to Ella's belief that 'no two skins are alike' you had to understand the individual skin conditions to treat the problems. The cells of the skin were the beginning of all life forces. They became Dixie's life work.

Empowering others

The business grew and the customers' intrigue also grew. As a result of Dixie's love for communicating her knowledge about the skin and skin products the Ella Baché College of Skin & Beauty Therapy was born. The college is a thriving business today. Education continues to be a fundamental part of our business, and we have the privilege of educating hundreds of students each year who learn about the skin, techniques, treatments, products and how to run a successful business. The graduating diploma students are revered as the best in the industry and go on to work both here in Australia and overseas. Advancements in technology have also allowed our students to learn all their theory online if they choose to, and then complete their practical classes in one of the training centres across Australia. To be part of the students' journey is very special. Quite often observing many of them on their first day, full of anticipation, self-doubt and many with bad skin, they quickly make lifelong friendships, and grow in confidence with knowledge, expertise and healthy skin. It's amazing how much having healthy skin is linked to greater confidence and self-esteem.

Graduation is one of my favourite nights of the year, watching the camaraderie and close friendships that have been made throughout the year, the confidence that has been found, and the pride in themselves for finishing their biology, anatomy assignments and theses on the skin. The common comment from many graduates is that the course is a lot more scientific and challenging than they had expected. This experience is only the beginning of their journey in an industry full of so many different opportunities. Many of those students have gone on to become businesswomen in their own right and have a lifelong partnership with Ella Baché. I can't help but think just how proud Dixie would have been.

★ ★ ★

The Ella Baché business became one of the largest skincare companies in Australia in the 1980s. And my grandma Dixie was one of the pioneers of the beauty therapy profession in Australia! Her success was due to her inquiring mind, love of what she did, passion for people and hard work. She had never agreed with the queen bee/working bee divide between people and had always resented those who insisted on having rights without taking on the obligations that came with them. Both my grandma and Ella were creators and inventors, and they didn't suffer fools easily!

Ella and Dixie both taught me about skin health—the functionality and biological makeup of my own skin and what I need to use to ensure it's healthy. They told me I needed to be grateful about the skin I was born with (I always wanted to be more tanned as a teenager), protect it and also make the most of it and not to get caught up in fads and trends as they come and go—to stay true to what I believed in and own my skin with confidence.

Not regretting how you look after your skin is only one part of living a fulfilled life. We'll look at other ways to live a life true to yourself in the next chapter.

BE BOLD
AND OWN YOUR SKIN

Do you look after your skin as well as you should? Try some of these tips for owning the skin you're in.

* Be confident in your own skin, and don't try and erase your individual beauty. Just enhance it.

* Understand and learn about your own skin's needs. They will be completely different from those of your friends.

* Start a daily skincare routine with good products and ingredients that work. It's as important as brushing your teeth.

* Trends come and go. They are not always here to stay, so back your beliefs and stand firm.

* Protect your skin from the sun: it's not only the best form of anti-ageing but too many people still die from sun-related cancers.

* Everyone's skin is unique; you need to nourish, protect and repair it, but you also need to own it on a deeper level and be yourself.

TALKING BOLD AND OWNING YOUR SKIN
WITH TRACEY SPICER

t was wonderful to sit down with journalist and advocate Tracey Spicer. In 2017 Tracey released her autobiography and gave a well-known TED Talk 'The Good Girl Stripped Bare'. Tracey talks about stripping back the layers to really own your skin and live your truth.

★ ★ ★

I worked at Network Ten. I was sacked after returning from maternity leave. It was then that I had to make a life-changing decision: should I sign the press release to say I had chosen to leave for family reasons (which would have been an absolute lie) or should I take the bold step of taking Ten to the federal court? The latter would start a national conversation in the media about pregnancy discrimination (which was affecting one in two women in the Australian workplace)—and that's exactly what I did.

I don't actually see myself as a courageous person, nor did I ever see myself as that bold person. Growing up I was always very much the 'good girl' not wanting to cause waves—just study hard, do well at school, be the good daughter, and be the good friend, all of that kind of stuff. Whenever I made a move it was like I had this thing inside me that once she shook off the shackles of being the good girl, motivated by seeing injustice and wanting to do the right thing, there was simply no other choice but to take action.

I still occasionally get crippled by the 'good girl syndrome', even though I was brought up by a non-sexist father and have an equalist husband and a feminist son. I tend to still slip back to old habits of all the years working in the male-dominated media, which meant not expressing your opinion. It's hard to break that habit of a lifetime, of being the passive woman who listens and supports others' opinions, rather than putting your own forward. You have to consciously break out of it.

It's the fire in the belly that drives me. Personally knowing women who fought hard in the 1960s and 1970s against inequality drives me to continue to fight hard, but also celebrate how far we have come in such a short time. Feeling overwhelmed by the insurmountable fight, just walking one foot in front of the other creates momentum. I am a founder and advocate for the not-for-profit organisation NOW Australia, which aims to raise awareness of and funds for victims of sexual harassment and assault. Just by biting off one thing at a time, even though I had never started a charity before, I gathered women using passion and social media in a positive way to build a powerful tribe organically by reaching out to people I knew. People say 'yes' more often than they say 'no'. It's really lovely.

Setting boundaries is hard but essential, especially when you're an advocate for sexual harassment. Technology is a wonderful thing, but it can easily creep into your life. Putting time limits on it, getting out, going for a walk and not letting it control you are all important.

I learned to not get overwhelmed. I have to manage any anxiety and predisposition towards panic attacks, but it doesn't happen very often these days. I really have to go into a quiet spot and do some deep breathing to get out of the fight or flight about getting up on stage, talking about a thorny issue or taking questions that might be adversarial. Making yoga a part of my daily life helps to not get a visceral physical reaction to anxiety and panic. Breathing and mantras also help to get out of that state of lack of confidence. But the most powerful thing I learned was to be able to breathe through whatever is stopping you in your head from really living that bold life.

The difficult part was breaking through the conspiracy theories caused by damaged self-esteem from what happened through all those years in the media, and being treated as someone who was valued for their appearance rather than what was in their heart or their head—someone who was valued for their diminishing currency of beauty rather than their brains. This still surfaces when I talk to media executives and bosses. I get these thoughts in the back of my mind that they're just looking at me and thinking, 'Oh, well, she's worthless because she's no longer young and beautiful'. And that's why I did a TED Talk, just to break down how damaging that is, particularly in the workplace and among young women in society when they're valued for their appearance. It really damages your self-esteem to the point where you think that's all people are thinking about when they're talking to me. I find mantras really do help me to get past that.

Thanking women such as Beyoncé for coming out there and saying, 'I'm not bossy, I'm the boss'. I just love these wonderful third- and fourth-wave feminists who embrace the idea of being an outspoken force—bossy, pushy women embracing that and saying, 'Well, yes, I am and so what? What is wrong with that?' We've really got to stop apologising for those terms and embracing them, I think.

I've lived most of my life as the good girl, feeling very constrained and incredibly under-confident, but the best thing I ever did was to speak my mind. And once you do it, once you embrace the boldness within, you will feel that you are unshackled, that you are happy, that you are confident. You know, it really does change your life embracing that boldness within. I never had as much support from my family, my friends and society as I have since I spoke my truth. And particularly in a world that's full of fake news and inauthenticity, people are seeking honesty. So use your words and your actions as an example to those around you, and you will never feel yourself as supported as you are in that moment.

Own your power. It feels fantastic!

Chapter 7
OWN YOUR LEGACY

The souls of men are not measured by what they have done,
but by what they leave behind.
Anonymous

I recently saw an interview with Terri Irwin where she said, 'We all have a legacy and the way you leave your life is the life you lead'. Terri moved countries because she fell in love and just as quickly it was taken away from her when her husband Steve died tragically in 2006. She has obviously thought very deeply about this experience and the legacy we leave.

So, what do you want your life to have been when you're sitting in your rocking chair and telling your story to the next generation?

To live a bolder and better life while we are on planet Earth it is worth knowing the two most common realisations people have when they are dying, according to Australian nurse Bronnie Ware, who worked in palliative care and wrote the book *The Top Five Regrets of the Dying*. First: 'I wish I'd had the courage to live a life true to myself, not the life others expected of me'. As Brené Brown once said, 'Owning our story can be hard but not nearly as difficult as spending our lives running from it. Embracing our vulnerabilities is risky but not nearly as dangerous as giving up on love and belonging and joy—the experiences that make us the most vulnerable'. So we need to step into the difficult and tough times to really experience the ability to live boldly. It's easy to imagine how many dreams have gone unfulfilled when you read Ware's book. Most people have not honoured even half of their dreams, always waiting for life to begin and having to die knowing that their regrets are due to choices they had made, or not made. People always like to think they will live longer than they do, that they have plenty of time left on the planet to fulfil their dreams. Time runs out for all of us. The time is now. It's a hard thing to master. If you had to write your own eulogy, what would you say? Don't wait for a rainy day or tomorrow.

The second wish of the dying according to Ware is, 'I wish that I had let myself be happier'. This is a surprisingly common realisation. But the truth is that you can choose to be happy or not. It's sometimes easier to stay with the familiar because, as they say, 'old habits die hard'. Fear of change can also make it hard to choose to be happy, as can pretending that you're content so others can't see that you're not.

The expression 'you have to get yourself out of the way' always rings true for me. We are our own worst enemy, and I think this is especially true for women. I often hear 'I'll do it once I have finished this course' or 'once my kid starts grade 3' and so on. I have come to learn that there is never a

Time runs out for all of us ... Don't wait for a rainy day or tomorrow.

perfect time and sometimes you get not what you want, but what you need, so jump in and back yourself—or at least pretend to!

Being free

In my twenties I travelled a lot with friends across pretty much every continent on the globe. There was total freedom and it was before 9-11, terrorism, mobile phones or any of the constraints and fear we deal with today. The thing that struck me was how much synchronicity came into our lives because we were open and free. Like bumping into someone you hadn't seen for years in the middle of an island in Thailand and spending a few weeks with them.

Or when you have nearly run out of money but you trust everything will be okay and someone accidentally overpays you from a previous contract in London. Or when you have just travelled on an overnight train from Berlin to Prague and get stopped by the guards at the border for not having a visa (which you didn't realise you were meant to have). So you walk for eight hours to arrive at a train station, and you come across a police officer who offers you a lift to where you want to go and doesn't look at your passport.

Cool, amazing stuff happens when you are open and you trust. The challenge is to remain this open when you get older and have the responsibilities of kids, work and everything else. I try to be spontaneous and free with my kids because I believe that's where the fun and magic happens. I have to be a planner and organiser at work so in my own time I love to just go with the flow. We do it in little ways, like simply walking out the front door (much to my husband's dismay, leaving it open most of the time) and heading off to the beach to go exploring. Kids teach you and remind you to be in the moment, and take pleasure from simple things. We walk around the rocks and I push my older son out of his comfort zone to stretch him. He is a deep thinker and likes to work everything out in his mind before he does it, whereas my little guy is more like me: jump and then figure it out later. You need both types of people in this world and with my work I have learned to be a lot more disciplined and analytical, to support my intuition and conceptual thinking. I am a 'glass half full' person. I think this has got me through the challenging times—I know the sun always shines tomorrow and the opportunities never stop coming.

Kids teach you and remind you to be in the moment, and take pleasure from simple things. I recently heard Dr Munjed Al Muderis' talk on legacy and dying. What an amazing human he is! He said that you can leave three things behind when you die. First, the knowledge of what you have learned; second, your legacy through your children; and third, making a difference. As a mum it's incredible to watch your kids learn and take on your legacy and what you teach them every day. Also, as a daughter I am grateful for what my parents, consciously or unconsciously, have passed down to me.

Being happy

The longest research study in the world on happiness is recorded in a TED Talk by Robert Waldinger called 'What makes a good life?' It's based on a Harvard University study of two groups of men in Boston. One group had attended Harvard University and the other group had not, with some of the latter even living on the streets. The study has been going for over 70 years. Men have died of drug overdoses and been killed in wars. Among the original recruits was John F. Kennedy, who went on to be president of the United States and do remarkable things. These men were surveyed every year from the study's inception and it was found that of those who are still alive today, it didn't matter which group the men were from — the answer to the question 'What makes a good life?' was the same: *the quality of my close relationships*. It's not about how much money you have; it's not about how hard you worked; it's about the quality of your close relationships. I know for myself, if I have conflict in my close relationships it creates stress in life. I am fortunate that I have lots of close relationships, and they have always been really important to me, no matter how busy my life has become. I do wish I had more time to foster new relationships, as so much happiness comes from getting to know people closely.

Being kind

My family always taught me to be kind and think about others. It often wasn't what they said, it was what they did. My mum would show it by driving to the moon and back for someone. She would always just show up in a time of need. The year I became CEO, I lost all the points on my driver's licence, which ultimately meant I couldn't drive for six months. This meant my usual 20-minute trip to and from work would take an hour

It's not about how much money you have; it's not about how hard you worked; it's about the quality of your close relationships.

and a half. Every day I would walk out of work and Mum would be waiting there in the car to drive me home. No matter how many times I told her not to turn up, she would always be there the next day. I soon realised there was little point arguing with her. But then I had to tell her to wait around the corner as it was a little embarrassing for someone in their early thirties who had just been appointed as a CEO to be picked up from work by their mum every day! It turned out that it gave us 30 minutes each day to talk and spend valuable time together.

Mum spent a lot of time with my kids. She would always say to them, 'you have one job in life and that's to look after each other'. Now that she is no longer there, my kids and I often repeat this to each other and I know they will remember this lesson from their grandma of being kind to each other for the rest of their lives. My dad, on the other hand, would always help others by having an open door for people in need. We would often have a house full of people. Some people would stay for a few hours; some for months and months. There were many nights when Dad was away, and I was still living at home, where one of his friends had broken up with his wife or was in between houses, so I would share the house with them. At first I would often dread it, but looking back I have had some fascinating conversations with people I would not have otherwise had the chance to talk to. It also gave me the ability and confidence to talk to anyone from a young age.

My husband Michael sometimes struggles with this open-door policy and drop-ins. I remember once he came home and called me because there was a man wearing his Speedos in our kitchen making himself a cup of tea. Bless him for having learned to accept—though maybe not yet embrace—the differences and quirks of my family. The one word that people use to describe my parents, for different reasons, is 'kindness'. I especially heard this when Mum passed away and I received so many beautiful letters from people — every single letter had the word 'kindness' in it.

My son recently won a school award and I was invited to attend the assembly to watch him receive the award. I didn't know what it was for and he didn't know I was in the audience. The look on his little face was priceless when his name was called out and he went up on stage to receive the award. It was for being kind to his friends. His smile was beaming from ear to ear. So was mine. I watched as his friends congratulated him with pats on the back and hugs. It was the best award he could receive. I was so proud.

Planning your legacy

Thinking about your own mortality, life and legacy is one of the hardest things to do. How many people set out to plan their life goals and what they want out of life, each year, right to the end of their life? I know people who do this and have concrete 30-year personal plans. I plan in the business, but I find having personal concrete plans hard, and in my view I need to leave life open to living and for the magic to happen.

What I do know about my life and legacy is that I want to be known as having been the best mum I could for my kids and to give them the best opportunity to live a happy and fulfilled life. I'd also like to help people through my work, especially young women who come in contact with the Ella Baché brand and network, by providing them with an opportunity to learn, grow and set up a good life for themselves.

BE BOLD
AND OWN YOUR LEGACY

What would you like your legacy to be? Try some of these tips for owning your legacy.

* Don't spend too much time trying to make others happy. Your happiness is your own.

* Spend more time with people you love; it is one of the biggest contributors to happiness.

* Life is shorter than we all think, so make the most of it.

* You can't control what happens in your life but you can control how you respond to it.

* Spend quality time with your kids as they are a big part of your legacy.

* Define your legacy now, as it's how you live your life.

* Try and live in the moment, and spend less time worrying about something that may never happen.

* Live outside your comfort zone—that's where the greatest learnings and magic happen.

TALKING BOLD AND OWNING YOUR LEGACY
WITH KIT WILLOW

Kit Willow is one of Australia's leading sustainable fashion designers. After launching her new label, KitX, in 2015 and exiting her first label, Willow, Kit is now changing the fashion game once again with the belief that 'every design decision has an impact on the planet and its people'.

When KitX began, 'sustainable fashion' was a daggy term. Kit has disrupted that view to create beautiful, desirable fashion that looks great and is sourced from sustainable materials. Creativity, kindness, integrity and transparency are at the heart of Kit's story as she pioneers this much-needed groundswell movement to sustainability. Here's Kit's story.

★ ★ ★

That fear, your fear, don't let it stop you from your actions and acting on your beliefs. You have got to be crazy and a little bit mad when making bold decisions; it takes serious amounts of passion and inner strength. When you believe, and believe strongly, you lose the fear and then the passion begins to drive you forward.

I have never sat down and tried to work myself out, but I know I made decisions and was prepared to own them every step of the way. When I look back at my 23-year-old self I wonder 'why lingerie?' I had no experience and it's the hardest category to develop, so for me that was bold. Stepping up and saying *yes* to doing a show in London on a shoestring budget with absolutely no money and not even shoes—cue: I had to beg, borrow and steal from my friends in London—was also bold. Leaping at the opportunities that were presented to me although not knowing how I was going to deliver is where I found my growth. I had an ignorance that, with time, grew into confidence.

When I started Willow I was very young, and I had a lot of incredible people around me on the journey. But then, towards the end, I went into partnership with new business partners and our values were misaligned. I lost my innocence through that experience. The values of the people around you, on every level—from suppliers to business partners, to friends—are important. Being able to align yourself with people with like-minded values is front and foremost and the best way to build a business, build a tribe and live your life.

After losing Willow, there was a huge shift for me, and it really forced me to be confident in my own skin and believe in what I was saying. I had to really learn to stand up and become assertive. Like I said earlier, once you have the belief you lose the fear and the only way becomes forward.

In my later years, after splitting with my husband and starting KitX, I had to make very hard and tough decisions, but I had to trust the journey and everything that I had worked for thus far—and when that all-too-familiar feeling of overwhelm creeps in I remind myself 'this will pass'. There's a quote I love and I remind myself of it often: 'sometimes when I'm waiting for the whenever, I just wait and the whenever comes to me'. For me this rings true to how I practise life. I allow myself to let go and trust good karma, and of course work hard. Finding the balance can feel like a constant battle, but I like to think it's a part of our journey.

There are always so many people to be thankful for, backing you and allowing you to be free and creative—to me they're angels.

The more I learn about the planet, climate change and the impact we are having on it, the more I want to share. I have spent time with leading scientist Tim Flannery from Climate Council. He has talked me through climate change, backed by scientific information. It's mind blowing but I am hoping that I will be able to share it using a wider audience and creating a positive change. The fire burning in my belly revolves around our planet and I have shifted my focus to new opportunities and materials coupled with strong design, hoping to make an impact the best way I know how.

To keep myself grounded I make sure I connect myself with the earth every day and I do yoga once a week. My children also keep me level. Spending time with them indulging in their conversations is my sanctuary and as long as they're healthy and happy then the rest will work. It's funny how much children just put your whole life into perspective.

When it all feels too much? I re-draw my thoughts and think about great things I have read; for instance, artist Georgia O'Keeffe once remarked 'Every day ... Every day ... Fear stricken every single day' and you know what? She doesn't let it stop her from doing what she does. As the age-old saying goes, diamonds are only formed in the harshest of conditions.

HOW DO YOU CREATE MOMENTUM?

So if you are up for celebrating and living a bold life, and finding joy in the ordinary and extra-ordinary moments, take some tips from my great-aunt Ella and the other amazing women in this book. Find your passion, push through your fears and self-doubt, step up, stand up and start playing at a higher level—not for profit, but for your own happiness. It all starts with those first steps.

Just pick a few things, do them well and commit to stop doing some things that you can let go of. I would encourage you to say *yes*. Experiment, and have fun along the way. And remember to laugh because you are going to stuff up somewhere on the journey. This is where the greatest lessons come from, even though they are tough at the time. Creating momentum is about taking that first step and showing up day after day, even if you simply start with one hour a day. It's going to require a lot of focus, hard work and commitment.

Time is such a precious commodity and we are all guilty of blaming our busy lives for not getting started. I'm best in the morning, so I get started from 7 to 8 am. Most of this book was written before 7 am. When I realised I had to run a business, look after my family, spend time with my friends and make sure I exercise ... oh, and write a book in three months ... the only way I was able to achieve momentum was to carve out an hour a day and keep going at it, day after day after day. Some days I sit and it just flows; other days I have nothing. But the focus and the discipline have helped me to create the momentum to get it done. I'm an extrovert and I therefore get my energy from others. I know I work best when I collaborate with others on projects. Quite often I will meet a friend or colleague for coffee and ask for their help to get my ideas down on paper and into a framework that I can use to set an end goal. Only you can make it happen and you have to start somewhere. That somewhere is best when it's baby steps—and by chunking it down, things won't feel like such an enormous, impossible task.

Learning new things and educating yourself will give you momentum and motivation. You are not expected to know it all or do it all. The world is changing at such a fast rate that we need to continue to educate ourselves and learn new ways of doing things. This is not always about signing up to a two-year MBA. It's often about reading a blog, an article or a book to learn new information and get exposed to different ways of approaching things. I learn from people around me every day.

How many times have you been stuck on something, but if you just 'sleep on it' you wake up in the morning with a lot more clarity and the ability to solve the problem that seemed unsolvable the day before? While I'm not an expert on sleep and the mind, I have had enough practice to know that sometimes it's better to wait, sleep on it and let your unconscious mind solve the problem. Try it.

Life isn't always easy. Perseverance and persistence are about trying to solve difficult things and hanging in there. I have come to realise that the law of gravity is often at play. Things always take longer than you think they will. So keep going and it will pay off, sometimes not in the form that you expect it to, but in the form you generally need it to. I love hearing about people doing phenomenal things, whether they are sports stars or founders of a company. You hear about their wonderful achievements and they are often presented as overnight successes. Overnight successes actually come in the form of 16 years or even 60 years. Nothing is ever an overnight success. Luck definitely plays a role in people's success. But it's about being able to pick the opportunities along the way and backing yourself. Don't let self-doubt stop you from picking those moments.

One of my colleagues has a great way of approaching things. He re-frames everything from the negative to the positive, so he always starts with a positive. For example, rather than saying to your child, 'Don't drop that pen on the floor', why not say, 'You're so great at putting your pens away'? We are all only human after all, and we spend a lot of our time solving problems—at home, at work, with the family—so if you have negative thoughts or a negative approach to something you have to do, then turn it on its head and re-frame it. It's amazing how different the outcome will be.

I am privileged to work with many people who have been at Ella Baché for more than 30 years. I often get asked in an interview with a new employee about the longevity of the people in the organisation. And while there are new people and young people here, there are many who have been here since I was in primary school. Their commitment is beyond one of work; they are so loyal, believe in the purpose and fabric of the organisation and treat it like their own. This is irreplaceable. It's about belief in the brand, company and people. They go above and beyond every day to make things happen and to get the outcome for the customer. I love hearing the stories of going above and beyond to make sure our customers are delighted. This has often meant our warehouse manager driving a product to someone's store or even to their house.

Have the courage to live a bold life: one that makes you happy and fulfils your passion!

You simply can't do it alone; you need to muster up support and win the hearts and minds of others to come along on the journey with you. I have also had to learn that sometimes people just won't make that journey—they simply don't want to, or it's not right for them—and that's okay. You can try and bring people along with you, but at the end of the day it's their choice if they jump on board or not.

I often have so much to do and achieve in any given week, so I try and chunk it down and take each day as it comes. Life's a marathon; running a business is a marathon. I must be a slow learner as I run every day like it's a sprint! This has its positives as I can get a lot done without it feeling overwhelming, but I often run out of gas by Thursday as I have already run four 100-metre sprints in the days leading up to it.

And, most importantly, have the courage to live a bold life: one that makes you happy and fulfils your passion!

HOW DO
YOU CREATE MOMENTUM?

* Carve out time for it, even if it's an hour a day.

* Chunk it down into small pieces; that way it doesn't feel like such a big, impossible task.

* Don't get caught up on perfection; just start and it will evolve.

* Focus, focus, focus.

* Laugh at your mistakes. You will learn from them.

* Learn everything you can. Education moves you forward.

* Pick the time of day when you are at your best.

* Re-frame things, and start from a positive.

* Remove your fears of failure.

* Solve it in your sleep.

* Work with others—collaboration creates momentum.

I hope you have enjoyed learning about Ella Baché: the person, the product and the brand. I have enjoyed reflecting on the generations before me, as well as interviewing some incredible Australian women who really are living bold lives, as I continue to drive this wonderful brand forward into the future, and continue the legacy, working with wonderful people and creating a positive impact on people's skin and the confidence that it gives you. I hope this book propels you to write your own story in life—to celebrate your skin and the story it tells—by loving and making the most of what you have and being in control of your own destiny.

INDEX

Throughout this index, 'PH' indicates 'Pippa Hallas', 'EB' indicates 'Ella Baché' (PH's aunt) and 'DH' indicates 'Dixie Hallas' (PH's grandmother)

cherish women's cancer foundation

Cherish Women's Cancer Foundation is a nationally registered not-for-profit organisation based in Brisbane, Queensland, Australia. Founded by Professor Andreas Obermair in January 2012, Cherish was established to generate funding for research and clinical trials that could be developed and implemented quickly to find kinder ways to treat women with gynaecological cancer.